A Bedside Book of Saints

Fr. Aloysius Roche

A Bedside
Book of Saints

SOPHIA INSTITUTE PRESS®
Manchester, New Hampshire

Sophia Institute Press®
Box 5284, Manchester, NH 03108
1-800-888-9344
www.sophiainstitute.com

Nihil obstat: Thomas McLaughlin, S.Th.D., *Censor Deputatus*
Imprimatur: Joseph Butt, *Vicarius Generalis*
Westminster, March 30, 1934

Library of Congress Cataloging-in-Publication Data

Roche, Aloysius, b. 1886.
    A bedside book of saints / Aloysius Roche.
        p. cm.
    Includes bibliographical references.
    ISBN 1-933184-08-6 (pbk. : alk. paper)
    1. Christian saints. I. Title.

BX4655.R6 2005
235′.2 — dc22   2005016901

05 06 07 08 09 10 9 8 7 6 5 4 3 2 1

To my parishioners —
who, with me, have spent
so many happy Sunday evenings
in the company of the saints

Contents

Preface

If there is to be a bedside book of saints at all, it ought to be made to look the part; its pattern may well be that of the old-fashioned quilt — a thing of threads and patches. Perhaps those quaint counterpanes of our grandmothers were designed on purpose to relieve the monotony of the bedroom and to give the sluggard or sick person something more interesting to look at than the tiresome white of the ceiling and sheets. So, these odds and ends have been sewn together without too much study and with very little plan, in the hope that they may be of service to an invalid here and there, and to those whose bad habit it is to read themselves to sleep. These chapters are not very heavy, certainly, so that they can be taken up without fatigue, at leisure, and even in drowsy moments.

But is it "quite the thing" to read pious books in bed? Listen to St. Jerome, one of the Fathers and Doctors of the Church: "Let holy reading be always at hand. Sleep may fall upon thee as thou lookest thereon, and the sacred page meet the drooping face."

Nor must it be forgotten that when we are in bed, things have a strange knack of looking different, like the view one gets of the land from a boat. Therefore we have tried to contemplate the

saints not from a new, but at least from a less familiar angle; moreover, from a comfortable angle, in order to give this book some of
the coziness it ought to have. In short, we have tried to bring the
saints near, to bring them home, to bring them to the very bedside.

And they will do most of the talking. "I am like a parrot who
has learned to speak," wrote St. Teresa. Exactly! These are our sentiments. But whoever is doing the talking, the talking will not be
too loud. It would never do to send you off to bed with a book about
the saints of the sort that is calculated to keep you wide awake all
night. And if a book of this kind is to have a sponsor, St. John of
God might do, because his emblem is a bed; or St. Vitus, because he
is the advocate of those who find it difficult to rise in the morning.

And finally, let us, writer and reader, make our own the beautiful prayer with which Mabillon ends his researches into the lives
of the saints: "May it please God not to impute it to me as a crime
that I have passed so many years studying the acts of the saints,
and yet resemble them so little."

In conformity with the decree of Pope Urban VIII, dated
March 17, 1625, we declare that, if in the course of this work we
should give the name of saint to those not officially recognized as
such; and if we make mention of such facts and revelations as
might bear the character of the miraculous or prophetic, we do not
in any way presume to take upon ourselves to express, on either
persons or facts, a judgment that is reserved to the Church, nor in
any way whatsoever to forecast decisions that belong to her alone.

A Bedside Book of Saints

Chapter One

The Human Nature of the Saints

It is comforting to know that in all the saints there is quite enough of the human element to give a human interest to the story of their lives. History exhibits to us plenty of heroes who had very little humanity and some who had none at all. The poet Shelley once said rather inelegantly, "You might as well go to a ginshop for a leg of mutton as expect anything human from me." But the servants of God are not of that sort. They are very complete men and women. And this is one of the sources of their great attraction. We like to find ordinary things even in extraordinary people. We like to find weaknesses even in those who are strong. A marble-and-bronze type of heroism excites our astonishment, but it leaves our heart rather cold. Christian heroism, however, dwells in hearts of flesh. So far from destroying the innocent weaknesses of our nature, sanctity finds in them its strength and its beauty.

We may be sure that the fathers of the desert, the anchorites, and the solitaries, all "felt the wild bird's thrill of song behind the bars";[1] and that the cloisters and the hermitages, even in the most

[1] Cf. Li T'ai-po.

3

strenuous ages of monastic penance, were peopled not by phantoms, but by human beings like ourselves: speaking, thinking, and feeling as do we; "fed with the same food, hurt with the same weapons, subject to the same diseases, healed by the same means, and warmed and cooled by the same summer and winter."[2] Who would ever have suspected that St. Anthony the Hermit was one of the most *sociable* of men? Yet St. Athanasius tells us that he was.

It is only too true that many of the saints appear to us to be very shadowy. This may be the fault or the misfortune of their biographers, who either do not or cannot tell us what they were really like; or are so intent on exhibiting their supernatural virtues that they have forgotten or thrown into the shade the natural elements. Besides, the saints resemble a rich landscape or a work of art. They require to be studied. We do not "take them in" at a glance or even at first sight. Some reveal themselves more rapidly than others; but some of them seem to wear a look of reserve on their faces, and to know them takes time. The very name of St. Dominic suggests something formidable: we think of the dog with the lighted torch in its mouth; we think of the terrible hammer of the Albigenses. It surprises us to find St. Dominic, in his weary journey across the Alps, carrying in his pack some wooden spoons as a pleasant surprise for the nuns in Rome who were his very good friends.

Again, St. John of the Cross has been called the "Inflexible Saint" and the "Impenetrable Saint." Some of his writings convey the impression of a man buried within himself, walled up as in a sepulcher, and looking out at the world of sense with bloodstained and terrible eyes. But the letters that passed between him and St. Teresa show plainly that he was nothing of the kind. If there had

---

[2] William Shakespeare, *The Merchant of Venice*. Act 3, scene 1, lines 55-58.

not been a very human side to St. John of the Cross, St. Teresa could never have teased him, as she was in the habit of doing, or have found a nickname for him and chosen it from among the pagan philosophers.

St. Ignatius, too, appears upon the distant horizon as a figure rigid and unbending; but the character of St. Ignatius is full of the most delightful and attractive traits. He could dance, and he did once dance. He could play billiards, and he did play once for a wager and won. He was so fond of flowers that he would never pluck them.

Behind the failure of biography and behind the haze that always gathers about the distant past, we can be certain to find that human nature of ours which is pretty much the same in all men and in every age. St. Aloysius, in spite of all impressions to the contrary, must have been a most attractive person, considering that he completely won the heart of a man like St. Robert Bellarmine. The great charm of the old monastic chronicles lies in this: that they are human documents. They unfold before our eyes, indeed, a spiritual drama; but they enable us to see that the actors in it are real men, with the passions and weaknesses of men, albeit those same men are quite evidently making great efforts to become saints.

Again, the martyrdoms of the early Church, somehow or other, present themselves to our imaginations as things statuesque or even ethereal. We know that St. Polycarp and St. Sebastian were men; and we know that St. Agnes and St. Cecilia were women, but we fancy, for some reason, that the man or the woman in them was completely sublimated by the sheer ecstasy and exaltation of their sacrifice. Yet, the English martyrs were the same sort of martyrs as those of the Coliseum; and the Acts of the English martyrs show how surprisingly human they were.

Indeed, St. Perpetua's description of herself, as recorded in her own Acts, is a very human description. She tells us how she was sitting at table with her family when the officers of the Crown came to remove her to prison; how in prison, "I was terrified, for I had never been in such darkness before. We suffered greatly from the heat and from the insolence of the jailers; and what gave me most pain was that I hadn't my baby with me." When her father came and on his knees begged her to take pity on his grey hairs and submit to the Emperor, "I was ready to die of grief to see him in such a state."

Besides, the characters of the saints, like that of all great people, were many-sided, and even the best biography may stress one side at the expense of another. Perhaps this explains how it happens that a dozen biographies of the same saint may appear within the space of a few years, each one bringing to light something another has overlooked. In the Middle Ages, there were sixty-six lives of St. Patrick in circulation at one time.

In our day, we have new lives of saints constantly appearing, and each one is hailed as an improvement on its predecessor. In the life of St. Margaret Mary, published by the Visitation of Paray-le-Monial, reference is made to the erroneous ideas concerning the saint that have been fostered by her biographers — and those erroneous ideas nearly all relate to the human side of St. Margaret Mary.

How unjust it would be to describe St. Jane Frances de Chantal as "the mother who stepped over the prostrate body of her son"; or St. Paula as "the mother who sailed away to the East, leaving her distracted children on the shore"; or St. Aloysius as "the youth who never looked at his mother's face"; and so on. The truth is that all these saints had very affectionate and tender hearts, and whatever sacrifices they made, they suffered most intensely in making them.

The Human Nature of the Saints

St. Ignatius stood up to his neck in a frozen pond. St. Benedict rolled in thorns. St. Jerome struck his breast with a heavy stone. Bl. Angela of Foligno branded herself with a red-hot iron. These are incidents in the lives of saints, but they are not the sufficient keys to the characters of the saints. Merely to know that they did such things is not to know the saints. The value of such incidents lies in this: they reveal to us that the saints had to wrestle with the same human problem of sin and temptation that daily confronts us.

It sometimes happens that accounts of the extreme and the extraordinary leave half of the story untold. For example, St. John Chalybita, the solitary, is cited as an instance of the length to which the old-time ascetics carried the spirit of self-abnegation. Having spent six years in the desert, he was given leave to return home. On the way, he disguised himself as a beggar and, not being recognized, was driven by his mother from her door. He then went to live in a little hut nearby, preserving the secret of his identity. This is the story of St. John Chalybita, but it is not by any means the whole of the story. The sequel is this: After three years, our Lord appeared to him, telling him that his penance was over and bidding him reveal himself to his mother. Overjoyed, the saint sent for her, told her everything, and later died in her arms.

We know nothing of St. Simeon Stylites except that he lived on a pillar. Yet, probably he laughed heartily at himself sometimes. At any rate, one of the pillar solitaries has left behind quite an amusing account of his experiences. And moreover, we gather that St. Simeon himself was a man of very sound common sense. He approached his experiment with great caution and cunning. For some years, he tried himself out, so to say, on small pillars, until he came to be able to do fifty feet without feeling it. We also know that there was no fanaticism or eccentricity about him because, at a word from authority, he was prepared to pack his experiment up and put it away.

Yes, the character of the saints was many-sided, and St. Teresa of Avila is a very good example of it. She was impetuous and hasty, yet cool, calculating, and business-like. She was simple, and she was extremely shrewd. She would give the poor anything they wanted, yet woe to the tradesman who tried any of his "business" tricks with her convent. She was susceptible to indignation and natural aversions (when Prioress Beatrix was in disgrace, she couldn't bear to hear her name mentioned). Yet she had a most affectionate, exuberant, and even playful temperament. A recent writer compares her to a stainless but metallic lily, forged of wrought iron. "Those who suffer," he says, "have scant consolation to expect from her." This was the impression made upon him by reading her works.

How different, however, is the impression of her letters. Here is revealed the sympathy, pity, and truly maternal tenderness of this "Mother of the Church," and above all, here is revealed the real woman. She speaks freely of her aches and pains, likes and dislikes, vexations and antipathies; pokes fun at the Inquisition; invents nicknames for her friends and enemies; and, woman-like, excuses her bad writing by blaming the pen. "The butter tasted very nice, as it was sure to do coming from you. So I accept it on condition that you remember me when you have any more that is particularly fine, as it does me a great deal of good. The quinces, too, were delicious. In fact, it seems to me as though you had nothing else to do except to give me pleasure." It is doubtful if so much human nature was ever compressed into so small a letter.

That they suffered and were apparently glad to suffer is no sign that they did not feel. "Let me suffer or die," prayed one of them. The Little Flower did not know how she would ever become acclimatized to Heaven, "to a place where there is no suffering." They may have crucified their flesh, as did St. Paul, but they did not thereby numb and petrify it. Broken-hearted Niobe prayed to be turned into stone; but the saints never said prayers of that sort. They were not made of stone, and they had none of the stone-like qualities of Stoics, whose ambition it is "to feel all feeling die." If they felt the smart of trial less than we, that was because they faced it with greater courage and resolution.

To shrink from suffering is to suffer twofold. None feel the cold so much as those who go shivering at the very thought of the cold. Timidity and an overnourished imagination are real sources of suffering. To look our trials steadily in the face, to strip them of their false and exaggerated colors, is to diminish their torments by at least one-half. The saints were brave in this sense, and to this extent they suffered less than we; but they suffered. The Curé of Ars suffered at the hands of the Devil; but he even got used to the Devil.

Hard and heavy burdens, certainly, the saints did bind upon their own backs; but it would be a great mistake to suppose that they naturally enjoyed carrying them. For example, we are plainly told that it cost the Curé of Ars a hard struggle to rise morning after morning long before dawn, and that again and again he entered the confessional, which took so terrible a toll on his time and strength, with the greatest natural reluctance. While in the Tower, St. Thomas More confessed to Meg, "I am of nature so shrinking from pain that I am almost afraid of a fillip." When St. Joan of Arc was under examination, she protested that wild horses would not have dragged her from her peaceful home to do the work that she did if God had not called her. What a cry of pain came from the heart of St. Gregory when he was elected Pope! "God," he said, "has called me to this terrible conflict." Sozomen tells us that St. Athanasius fled and hid himself when rumor reached him that he might be nominated Patriarch of Alexandria. René Bazin thus describes the election of Pius X: "As soon as he saw that there was an increase of votes, he did his utmost to avoid the threatened dignity. 'Do not think of me,' he said. 'I have not the requisite qualities.' Later Msgr. Merry del Val was sent to ask if he intended to persevere in his refusal. He thought of looking for him in the Pauline Chapel . . . and there he was, kneeling on the pavement, his head bent, his face hidden in his hands, and the hot tears pouring down his cheeks."

One who has written well of the saints reminds us that "their souls are not the Dead Sea, which no breath of wind ever ruffles and where no life moves beneath the heavy weight of the waters. They are rather that Sea of Genesareth, which had many disturbances and storms and only grew calm beneath the Master's hand." In short, they had their full share of ups and downs, disappointments and difficulties.

> Many a blow and biting sculpture
> Polished well these stones elect;
> In their places now compacted
> By the Heavenly Architect.

They had their weaknesses, and their temptations; and they had their faults — faults that St. Alphonsus said he would be lucky to be rid of a quarter of an hour before his death. How irascible St. Francis de Sales was by nature! What a stiff battle he had to fight to master his temper! He is quite frank in telling us that the passion of anger was uncommonly strong in him and that he had to exert himself to the utmost to keep it down. The faults of St. Gertrude were so notorious that St. Mechtilde actually asked our Lord why He was able to love her so much. St. Francis of Assisi, who "did ever pay the highest heed that never should he be a hypocrite before God," made no secret of his temptations, and he confessed to his brethren that he *felt* vainglorious as often as he gave an alms. This simplicity is, in fact, one of the great notes of God's servants, and it means that they never played a part; never pretended to be other than they were; never countenanced the pretenses and poses of the worldly. It means, in short, that they were, above all, real and genuine — that is to say, natural and human. Affectation was St. Philip Neri's pet aversion.

How candid and engaging are the "confessions" of St. Thérèse of the Infant Jesus! She tells us about her aversions and repugnances; she admits that searching in books for beautiful prayers made her head ache, and that in the morning she felt no courage or strength for the practice of virtue. She was on the point of showing her annoyance to the Sister who splashed her with the dirty water in the laundry. She was sorely tried by the fidgeting of her neighbor at Meditation; and the effort she made to restrain her impatience "cost me so much that I was bathed in perspiration."

Or there is Clare Vaughan on her deathbed: "It is all very well to say, 'Courage, Clare, courage,' when one only sees Paradise through a little hole."

And here is what the *Mirror of Perfection* tells us of the last days of St. Francis of Assisi: "Whilst he was sick of the ailment from which he died, he one day called his companions, saying, 'You know how Lady Jacqueline of Settesoli was and is exceeding devoted unto me; and I do therefore believe that she would hold it a great consolation were we to notify her of mine estate, and specially send her word that she send me of the marchpane that many a time she hath made for me in the city.' " This marchpane, or marzipan, was a confection of almonds and sugar; and sure enough it was sent for and it came, although it happened to be on the way in any case.

Chapter Two

The Common Sense of the Saints

"The saints have liquid hearts": this is one of the sayings attributed to the Curé of Ars. The expression, however, comes from St. Thomas Aquinas. Perhaps St. John Vianney was a more deeply read man than has been commonly supposed.

Sanctity is certainly solid; that is to say, it rests upon a real foundation and is never a thing of mere moods and feelings. But with this real sanctity there is always associated a certain fluidity of soul, a liberty of action, a breadth of mind, and a pliability as well as a tenacity of will. It has that elasticity recommended by St. Paul: "All things to all men."[3]

There is nothing stiff or rigid or blindly unbending about true piety. It is this that fills the lives of the saints with surprises. We read a few chapters and set about making up our minds about the saints, when around the corner appears something quite unexpected and we have to make up our minds all over again.

When the Prefect of the Department went off to tell the Curé of Ars that the Emperor had conferred upon him the Cross of the

[3] 1 Cor. 9:22.

Legion of Honor, he no doubt felt pretty certain that the news would be received in the manner customary to saints. He must have been thunderstruck when he heard the good Curé asking, "Is there a pension with it?"

"What a shrewd mind that man had!" said René Bazin, with evident surprise. Indeed, nobody ever got really used to the Curé. People made a regular habit of going to Ars, and they always found something fresh. As a rule, the more often we approach a remarkable man, the less remarkable he appears. But St. John Vianney fairly turned this truism outside in.

We have already considered the many-sidedness of the saints and remarked that this makes their true portraiture a difficult task. It is not that they were several people rolled into one, but that they were adaptable, pliant, free from grooves, equal to all circumstances and occasions — in short, endowed with an uncommon amount of common sense.

As Fr. Faber said, "Holiness is a spacious thing." Holiness, in fact, is keenly alive to the actualities of life.

"We must adapt the Society [of Jesus] to the times, not the times to the Society," St. Ignatius said.

"It shows weakness of mind to hold too much to the beaten track through fear of innovations. Times change, and to keep up with them, we must modify our methods": this is how St. Madeleine Sophie writes in one of her letters. Pliable subjects were those she liked best. Finding herself short of novices at a time when her educational work was spreading, she prayed for them. "O God," she said, "give me saints." Saints, she knew, would be pliable and therefore useful tools.

One of the outstanding qualities in St. Vincent de Paul was just this: "His instinctive sagacity told him that the sun will neither stand still nor go back upon its course; that God fulfills Himself in many ways; that if we would shape the world better, we must begin by shaping ourselves to it as we find it."

When Thomas Carlyle first looked into the *Chronicle of Jocelin of Brakelond,* what astonished him was to find a deeply religious man like Abbot Samson abounding in practical sense. "Our abbot has a right honest feeling, without insolence and without fear or flutter, of what he is and what others are."

Among the depositions made by Mother Greyfié, the Superior of Paray, concerning St. Margaret Mary is this: "She was full of common sense."

The very name of St. Teresa of Avila speaks for itself. There is a sort of tacit understanding among us that she is the patron of common sense, the saint to whom those have recourse who are not too well endowed with that particular commodity. There was certainly no nonsense about St. Teresa. She sent humbug about its business by defining humility as truth: "Humility is truth." She had no time for pious stupidities or deceptions. She was well aware of her own powers and made no secret of either her virtues or her defects. She was rather sorry that she was not a man because if she had been, she would have been a priest and *therefore* an eloquent preacher. "Father Antonio," she writes, "is a saint, but God has given him no talent for ruling." On the other hand, she nominated a superior who was far from being a saint and when this was pointed out, she said, "'I know, I know; but still he is an able administrator."

When argument was going on about the habit of her new religious, she said, "Believe me, the question is not whether we are going to wear religious habits or not wear them, but whether we are going to practice virtue or not." St. Augustine long before had insisted on much the same thing: "A man's poverty before God is judged by the disposition of his heart and not by his coffers."

Mortified though St. Teresa was, she liked a room with a good view from the window; and when her eyes gave her trouble, she did the practical thing that apparently Pepys a hundred years later and in London could not or at least did not do: she invested in a good pair of spectacles. "When taking off her spectacles," we are told, "she fell into an ecstasy."

"If obedience," St. Teresa declared, "sends you to the refectory six times a day, go and be glad to go." This recalls the saying of St. Philip Neri: "Eat without scruple"; and again, "In general, give the body rather too much food than too little."

When St. Pascal Baylon was setting about a plate of fish that his superior had ordered him to eat, one of the Brothers affected to be a little scandalized. "Obedience," said the saint, "comes first, devotion second."

The teaching and spirit of St. Francis de Sales are on the same sensible level: "God wishes to be served with a reasonable service. It is always easy to reduce the bodily forces, but it is not so easy to build them up again. It is easier to wound than to heal. The soul should treat the body as its child, correcting without hurting it." "Have patience with everyone, but especially with yourself. He who has lost courage has lost everything." "We must be charitable to our own soul." "Be just; neither excuse nor accuse your own soul." And then this gem of good advice: "We must submit patiently to the trial of being human."

The like spirit was seen in St. Francis of Assisi. We are told that he was once wakened out of his sleep by one of the brethren calling, " 'I am dying of hunger.' Then the Blessed Francis had a table laid out and did eat with him, lest he should be ashamed to eat alone." St. Francis then preached a little sermon on the virtue of common sense. "Each one of you ought to pay heed unto his own nature."

The Common Sense of the Saints

It has been remarked of Samuel Johnson that he invested common sense with a kind of majestic sanctity. St. Francis de Sales invested sanctity with a majestic common sense. Indeed, it is difficult to read the Bishop of Belley's *Spirit of St. Francis de Sales* without thinking of Dr. Johnson. In the "Table Talk" of both there appears the same aversion to cant and affectation and snobbishness, and even at times a striking similarity of tone. Johnson was no saint, but in some ways he approached very closely to Catholic ideals; and he had, at any rate, one great virtue of the saints: common sense. St. Francis de Sales wrote to the Bishop of Belley, "Do you really want me to pretend that black looks exhilarate me and that I can bear smoke puffed in my face without sneezing?" St. John Chrysostom long before expressed the same sentiment: "Not to feel pleased at being praised is, I am inclined to think, what has never happened to any man."

Violent and extreme views were very distasteful to St. Francis de Sales. When some people were maintaining that great cities were hotbeds of temptation, he interposed, "The country has its drawbacks as well as the town. Just as there is good company and bad, so there is good and bad solitude. Solitude is bad if it is the sort of which it was said: Woe to him who is alone. Lot in the midst of a corrupt city was a good man. In the wilderness he fell grievously. There are many virtues that cannot be practiced in solitude. Some have been known to lose perfection in solitude and regain it in a busy city life. Wherever we are, we can aspire to the perfect life."

He defended the devout lady who wore earrings by saying, "We must remember that Rebecca had earrings." Man of routine though he was, he would put everything aside to give pleasure to his guests, and after lunch he would take them for a row on the lake. "Charity," he would say, "is never a waste of time." This reminds us of St.

Thomas Aquinas, who begins one of his letters, "Tonight I have given up my prayer in order to write to you."

Unlike the Curé of Ars, St. Francis had no objection to having his portrait taken or distributed. "There is no more harm in that than in communicating one's thoughts to one's neighbor; and if it gives him pleasure, it is an act of charity." Yet he never allowed his charity to get the better of his common sense. He writes to a lady friend who had a penchant for lawsuits, "Those who live at sea usually die at sea. The money these lawsuits of yours are devouring would be more than enough for you to live on."

A similar strength of mind appears in the letters of St. Bernard. He writes to his great friend and benefactress, the Duchess of Lorraine, "I salute the Duke, your husband, and I venture to urge him and you, if this castle for which you are going to war does not really belong to you, to leave it alone."

We may apply to the saints what a great French writer says of the Christians of the Middle Ages: "We must not think of them as a flock of pious sheep bleating and flying for protection to the knees of the shepherd, but rather as men armed with a very robust personality." How robust was the personality of St. Teresa of Avila and of St. Catherine of Siena! It is extremely doubtful if our age, with all its advantages, could produce anything approaching those types of women. Manly they never tried to be, because they had sufficient strength of mind to be real women; but about each there was something athletic and adventurous.

St. Catherine, like another Peter the Hermit, moved about rousing the public opinion of Italy. Some of her letters are like red-hot sparks struck off an anvil. "Fools that you are," she writes, "and worthy of a thousand deaths. You are so blind that you cannot see even your own shame." "I have heard," she writes to the Pope, "that demons in human form have elected an antipope against you. Now then, forward, Most Holy Father. Go into the battle without fear." She tells the Papal Legate to be a man and not a coward. She had so much to say to her director that sometimes he would fall asleep, but she roused him without any remorse saying, "Am I talking to the walls or to you?" She knew how to defend herself. When it became known that she passed long periods nourished only by her Holy Communions, one of the priests thought it a strange thing that she could not live like other people. At once she sent him a little note: "You say, Father, that I must pray particularly to God to be able to eat. And I say to you that I have prayed continuously and do pray and will pray that God may give me the grace to live like other creatures in this business of eating, if it is His will, because it is mine."

St. Catherine is very like St. Jerome. Like him, she was slandered, and like him, she refused to sit down under the slander. Man of retirement though the holy Doctor was, when evil tongues wagged about the good work he was doing, he came right out of his shell: "Have I ever taken money from my pupils? Have I not always repulsed every gift, large or small? Have I ever been known to utter a double-meaning word or to cast too bold a glance?"

One of St. Jerome's letters to Laeta, the wife of Toxotius, contains rules for the education of her little daughter. They are certainly very commonsense rules, and it is not easy to realize that they were drawn up more than fifteen hundred years ago:

Let her have an alphabet of little letters made of box or ivory so that she may play with them and in this way learn, while amusing herself. When she is a little older, let her try to form each letter in wax with her finger, guided by another's hand. Then, let her be invited, by prizes and presents suited to her age, to join syllables together. Let her have companions to learn with her, so that she may be spurred on by emulation and by hearing their praises. She is not to be scolded or browbeaten, if she is slow, but rather to be encouraged and made to feel sorry to see herself outstripped by others. The greatest care must be taken that she does not acquire a hatred of study, because such an aversion is very difficult to shake off. Her nurses must never allow her to chop her words; above all, she must be taught to speak her own language with the greatest correctness. She should at the same time learn to spin, weave, and make her own clothes.

At the other end of the fifteen centuries, we have a great educator like St. Madeleine Sophie. She was not only up to date in her methods, but was always on the alert for new ideas, and, with great strength of mind, she saw that they were carried out. She knew the world well, and although she herself had retired from it, she aimed at preparing her pupils to take their places in it without shrinking from its difficulties. In the midst of all her vexations and misunderstandings, she kept a level and a cool head. "No politics" was the peremptory order she issued to her superiors at a time when everybody in France was either a Legitimist or an Orleanist.

It has been said of St. John Berchmans that he was canonized for keeping his Rule. But it would be a mistake to think, as the world commonly thinks, that these Rules that the saints kept were no more than the mechanical regulations of monasteries and convents; and that the saints were wholly intent upon the petty observances of keeping silence and rising and going to bed at the appointed hours.

St. Benedict in his Rule insists that the monk's paramount duty is to uproot his vices. In the fourth chapter, called "The Instrument of Good Works," it is laid down, first of all, that God must be loved "with all our heart and soul and strength." "Then, to love our neighbor as our self." "Then, not to kill." "Then, not to steal." And so on through the commandments.

So, too, the author of the Ancren Rule[4] begins by reminding the Sisters that the first and most important of all rules is the rule of the heart, the regulation of our conduct according to the laws and commandments of God. All the other rules regulating food, drink, sleep, and so on are only bodily exercises and profit not at all except insofar as they direct the heart within. "The first rule is a lady; the others are her handmaids," he adds.

The seventh-century saint Eligius, or Eloy, insists upon the very same thing. There is extant a sermon of his around which a great controversy raged. In this sermon the saint lays down the rules of a Christian life. He does indeed speak of prayer and churchgoing and contributions to the service of the altar; but the chief burden of his discourse is this: "Love your friends in God, and love your enemies for God. Keep peace and charity; avoid lies; tremble at perjury; bear no false witness; commit no theft; visit the infirm; place the whole of your hope in Christ alone."

So far from being mainly interested in having ecstasies, St. Teresa tells us, "I have never presumed to desire that God should give me so much as the least tenderness of devotion. I begged only the grace never to offend Him."

Moreover, intent though they were on big things, the saints by no means neglected small behavior, as pious people are sometimes very apt to do. For example, it has been very rightly said of St. Francis of Assisi, "All are agreed that politeness flowed from him.

---

[4] A thirteenth-century code of rules for the life of anchoresses, sometimes called the Nuns' Rule.

If there was one thing of which so humble a man could be said to be proud, he was proud of his good manners." St. Teresa of Avila was quite fastidious in all that related to courtesy and good breeding. "God," she would say, "cannot bear our being ungrateful to those who have done us a good turn. A sardine would bribe me." It is related of St. Ignatius that as long as the men of rank who joined the Society of Jesus were novices, he made a point of addressing them by their titles. And of St. Philip Neri we are told that although he commanded the obedience of all, he never ordered anyone to do anything. It was always "Please" or "Would you mind," or "If I sent you to such and such a place, would you go willingly?"

And most surprising of all, we do not find that the saints were finicky people or sticklers for trifles. "Leave something for the angels," is what St. Philip Neri said to the overscrupulous priest; and he saw nothing wrong in high-heeled shoes, provided they did not trip up those who wore them. When St. Augustine was asked about the morality of overindulging the sense of smell, he answered, "About fragrant smells, I do not concern myself much except to welcome them in God's name when they are present."

"How am I to know whether or not I am praying properly?" someone asked St. Anthony. "By not knowing it," was the answer.

"Monsieur le Curé," said a child to St. John Vianney, "must I learn my lesson, or can I go out to play?" "Play, my child; it is the privilege of your age."

"Although we read," says St. Benedict, in his Rule, "that wine is not the drink of monks at all, yet since in our days monks cannot be persuaded of this, let us at least agree not to drink to satiety."

"Remember," says the Ancren Rule, "that everything may be overdone. Moderation is always best. You ought never, like unwise people, to *promise* to keep any of the external rules. You may even change them whenever you will for better ones."

Such was the level-headedness of the saints.

Simple they certainly were, but they were not simpletons. They were childlike, but not childish. They did not "put off the old man" in order to put on the old woman. St. Paul has summed it all up for us: "Do not become children in sense; but in malice be children and in sense be perfect."[5]

[5] 1 Cor. 14:20.

Chapter Three

⌒

The Affections of the Saints

It would be a mistake to think that because God's servants made heroic sacrifices and severed some very sacred ties, they must have had rather hard hearts or at least have been devoid of tenderness. But the love of the heart is not stifled or impaired by being dedicated to God; on the contrary, it is thereby purified and strengthened and thus rendered more delicate, and more energetic. "When the heart is pure," said the Curé of Ars, it cannot help loving, because it has rediscovered the source of love, which is God."

The Bretons claim to be French twice over — *deux fois français;* and holy people not only claim the right to love their loved ones, but, because they are holy people, they can claim to love them with a twofold love.

The passion of love can be disciplined without being destroyed. St. Francis de Sales had to discipline the passion of love, which, in him, was uncommonly strong. Indeed, he owns that the two passions that cost him most to control were anger and love. The first he violently repressed, but not so the second. With that he used strategy. He left his affections alone, infused into them a supernatural motive, and, by so doing, made them more ardent than ever.

Indeed, it is the undisciplined passion that is weak — so weak that it is short-lived as a rule. No man is a greater stranger to love than the libertine. "The real thing does not exist," such people say. Certainly it does not and cannot for them.

A modern French writer has described the effect upon himself of mixing in the irreligious society of his day. He tells us that it acted like a detergent upon his soul, purging it of all trustfulness and curing him of friendship in the winking of an eye. And was it not a woman of the world who described friendship as an "insipid sort of hatred"?

But religion does not disfigure the beautiful works of God. It does not even check the warm impulses of a generous affection; nor, as we shall see, does it stifle the tender accents of endearment. It adds; it does not take away. It enriches human love with the additional glory of being able to consecrate itself to the Source of all love.

Not only did the saints have hearts, but the genius of the saints is their good-heartedness. Menander, the Greek poet, said, "A rich heart is the chief thing that a man wants"; and the saints had this chief thing. Their hearts were very rich indeed. It was a saint (Anthony) who said, "To be a lover of men is to live." It was a saint (Augustine) who said, "Virtue is nothing but well-directed love." It was a saint (Francis de Sales) who said, "The soul cannot live without love. All depends on providing it with a worthy object."

Wordsworth speaks somewhere of the "defrauded lives" of those who devote themselves to the religious life. It never occurred to him, apparently, that those very lives are abundantly supplied not only with consolation, but also with the joys and sweetness of friendship and affection. St. Jerome and St. Basil would, no doubt, have satisfied Wordsworth's theory of the defrauded lives. Both made great acts of renunciation; and with neither is it easy for the imagination to associate what we call sentimentality. Yet it is only necessary to read their letters to see what tenderhearted and affectionate men they were. St. Jerome's name is rather suggestive of harshness or at least sternness; but he loved St. Paula, and he loved her whole family. He thus writes to her concerning her little granddaughter: "If you send her to me, I shall become her tutor and her nurse. I shall carry her on my shoulders, old man though I am, and hold lisping dialogue with her, prouder of my office than ever Aristotle was of his."

And St. Basil writes as follows to console a mother on the death of her child: "But what am I doing! I forbid a mother to weep, and yet I weep myself. I acknowledge it: the page on which I write is wet with my tears, and there are moments when I cry, 'Let the day perish wherein I was born.' "

Here is St. Francis de Sales writing to St. Jane Frances de Chantal: "Truly, there is not a soul in the world, I think, whose affection is warmer, more tender, and to speak quite plainly, more loving than mine; for it has pleased God thus to make my heart." Of his mother he wrote, "Oh, this mother of mine, how I am forced to love her!" When his sister Jeanne, whom he had baptized, died, he suffered intensely: "My heart has been touched more than I ever thought possible. Oh, how deeply I loved this little child!"

St. Teresa of Avila's love for her own flesh and blood was such that she acknowledged that the hardest thing she ever had to do was to leave her father. "My relations," she writes, "were extremely fond of me, and I loved them so much that I would never allow them to forget me."

What touching and tender things St. Thérèse of the Infant Jesus writes of her father. When he was stricken by paralysis, she said, "Even as the agony of Jesus pierced the heart of His Mother, so my heart was deeply wounded by the humiliations and sufferings of him whom I loved best on earth." And again, "I no longer said I could suffer more; words cannot express my grief, nor shall I attempt to describe it here." And then she writes of her sister, "What talks I had with Celine! Far from separating us, the grating of Carmel united us more closely."

What mother ever had a more affectionate son than St. Monica; and what son ever had a more affectionate mother than St. Augustine? Certainly, the memory of parents was never honored in more beautiful words than these: "Let her therefore rest in peace together with her husband. And inspire, O Lord my God, inspire Thy servants that so many of them as shall read these Confessions, may at Thy altar remember Monica Thy handmaid, together with Patricius, her sometime husband. May they with devout affection be mindful of these parents of mine; so that what my mother in her last words desired of me may be fulfilled for her in the prayers of many."

St. Jerome in his panegyric on St. Paula says, "No mother so loved her children." Although she parted from those children at the call of duty, her heart was torn asunder by the separation. Having settled her affairs and left her family well provided for, "she went to the waterside attended by her relations and children, who all strove by their tears to overcome her constancy. When the vessel was ready to sail, her little son Toxotius with uplifted hands begged her not to leave him. But she, raising her dry eyes to Heaven, turned her face from the shore, lest she should see what she could not behold without the most sensible pangs of sorrow." From this heroic woman God demanded a sacrifice but not a holocaust. If He willed that she should forgo the society of those dear ones, He did not will that she should love them the less. Indeed, He crowned the sacrifice that she made of her maternal instincts, by deepening and purifying the natural love of her heart, so that St. Jerome was able to say truly, "No mother so loved her children."

This is very clearly brought out by what is related of St. Severus of Ravenna. He was a poor weaver and a married man, but being a man of exceptional virtue, he was elected bishop. He accepted the decision as coming from God, and separated from his wife and daughter. Of both, however, he continued to take the tenderest care; and when they died, he had them buried in a splendid sepulcher. When he himself came to die, he had the sepulcher opened, and entering it, he lay down at his wife's side saying, "My dear ones, make room for me so that in death we be not divided."

Let us consider the two following examples side by side, and let us judge the quality of the affection in each case.

It is well known that if Lady More had had her way. Thomas More would not be one of the English Martyrs. "I marvel," she said when she visited him in the Tower, "that you, who hitherto have been taken for a wise man, will now so play the fool. . . . You have at Chelsea a right fair house, your library, garden. . . . There you might be in company of me, your wife. . . ." Lady More certainly loved her husband; but, as often happens, her love had a great deal of self-love in it. As Fr. Bridgett says, "She was evidently one of those good souls to whom respectability is the law of laws, and to whom a scruple to do what decent people do is simply unintelligible."

Now, by way of contrast, here is the wife of another martyr. In 1929, the Armenian Gomidas Keumurgian was beatified. He was a married priest and was beheaded by the Turks at Constantinople in 1707. The relation of his martyrdom tells us that although his sister endeavored to persuade him to embrace Mohammedanism and so save his life, his wife, on the contrary, exhorted him to constancy. When she heard that he had been condemned to death, she declared that nothing must shake his resolution, not even anxiety for the welfare of his children, for whom God would be sure to provide. (Indeed a pension was later settled upon the children by the Holy See.) This is love in its purest form, an affection superior to all self-interest and seeking only the welfare of the beloved object.

The Nevers life of St. Bernadette, by way of introducing some of her correspondence, says, "The religious life does not suffocate the affections; it elevates and intensifies them." And in the letters that follow, we have evidence not only of Bernadette's practical sense, but of the tender love she lavished upon the absent members of her family. "Separation from our beloved father is very distressing," she writes, "but we have the great consolation of knowing that he received the last sacraments." And again, "My dear Sister, I have felt a large part of the pain that your mother's heart endured in losing your little daughter." "I hear that my Aunt Lucile is very ill. Write, I implore you, and conceal nothing from me." "I assure you that at this moment, I am very much concerned about your future." "I am very much disturbed indeed concerning Pierre." "My dear Sister, I beg of you to let me have any news as soon as possible." And again and again, "Convey to the family a thousand affectionate things from me."

This is how St. Anselm writes to his relations: "Souls well beloved of my soul, my eyes ardently desire to behold you; my arms expand to embrace you; my lips sigh for your kisses; all the life that remains to me is consumed with waiting for you. How can I forget those whom I have placed like a seal upon my heart!"

The Affections of the Saints

St. Anthony, the patriarch of the monastic life, is certainly one of the greatest of the ascetics. St. Athanasius was his first biographer, and he tells us that Anthony did not retire to the desert until after the death of his parents. When that happened, his only near relation was his sister. This sister he placed in a nunnery. But he never forgot her, because in his old age he left his solitude to pay her a visit.

One of the most beautiful things in the *Dialogues* of St. Gregory the Great is his account of the last interview between St. Benedict and his sister St. Scholastica. She was in the habit of visiting her brother every year and conversing with him until evening at a house not far from the monastery. On the last occasion, knowing that she would never see him again in this world, she asked him to delay his return until the next day. St. Benedict replied that he could not possibly pass a night out of his cloister. She therefore had recourse to God; and He sent such a thunderstorm that St. Benedict was unable to put his foot out of the door until the following morning. "God forgive you, sister, what have you done?" "I asked you a favor, and you refused; I asked it of God, and He has granted it to me."

Even the virtue of patriotism was quite safe in the hands of the saints. Although so many of them were voluntary exiles from their native land, they felt and expressed their affection for it, an affection that our Lord consecrated by shedding tears over Jerusalem.[6] How sensitive of the good name of his country St. Boniface shows himself in the fearless letter he writes concerning Ethelbald, the immoral king of the Mercians! "Born and nurtured as we are of the same English race, we remain here abroad by the command of the Apostolic See. We are always glad and rejoice in the good

[6] Luke 19:41.

report of our nation; but by its sins we are distressed and saddened. We suffer from the disgraceful conduct of our people. If indeed the race of the English — as is noised abroad and is cast up to us in France and in Italy — spurn lawful wedlock, a people degenerate and unworthy will be born and the nation will cease to be strong. We suffer for the disgraceful conduct of our people."

Did not St. Francis bless Assisi with his dying hand? As his end drew near, he was carried from place to place in search of health, but he was homesick all the time. When at last the Brethren returned to Assisi, a great joy filled him at the sight of it. "Never give up this place," he said. "If you go anywhere, always return here to your home."

"O my native land," said St. Camillus of Lellis on his deathbed, "remember what I have taught thee, for we shall never see each other again."

When Pierre de Blois left the Abbey of Croyland, he stopped seven times to look back and fix upon his mind the memory of the place in which he had left his heart.

We are told of St. Philip Neri that, on the morning when he said his last Mass, "he gazed long at the well-known hill [the Janiculum] from which he would never again see Rome spread out in its majesty at his feet." "My country is Heaven," he was fond of saying; but, all the same, his biographer tells us, "Amidst the labor of his apostolate in Rome, he had never forgotten his beloved Florence or his relations; his affection for both was sanctified and ennobled by his ardent love of God." He never missed an opportunity of befriending any needy fellow-countryman (i.e., a Florentine); and to one of his relations he writes, "I need not offer you my services because the ties of relationship bind me to aid you. Such as I am, I will always gladly do anything in my power for you, loving you as I do and being, by age and by relationship, as a father."

The Affections of the Saints

Grace is never the effacement of nature, but rather its embellishment. Sanctity transfigures earthly love so that the shape of its countenance is altered and its very "garments become white and glittering."

Chapter Four

⁓

The Lives and Letters of the Saints

If we had as many letters as we have biographies of saints, our appreciation of the saints would grow, and we would be rid, once for all, of the wrong impressions we have formed of some of them. St. Augustine says, "As the eyes are to the other senses, so are the letters of illustrious men, in numberless ways, more wonderful than all their other works. In them, as in the mirror of the human eye, appear the personal qualities of the individual. No one can better show himself to the life than in his letters. Nowhere can he be better known."

Biographies there must be, and in many cases there is nothing else; but there is just so much that the best biographer can do and no more. He can use only the materials that lie to his hand, and they may be very scanty. It would be difficult to write a really good biography of St. George. And since the biographer has the handling of the materials, such as they are, he must handle them in his own way. In spite of himself, he will be biased in the selection of his facts. He is the judge of what is noteworthy and what not; and naturally he will emphasize what appeals to his own mind. His very erudition may be his undoing, because he will be apt to bring forward only what appeals to his own scholarly judgment.

A Bedside Book of Saints

If Boswell had been a brilliant man, we would never have had *the* life of Samuel Johnson. Prior was all that Boswell was not; but Prior, in his *Life of Goldsmith*, walks on stilts, while Boswell, in his *Life of Johnson*, walks with his feet on the ground. We are always grateful for a brilliant study of a saint — for example, Gheon's *Secret of the Curé of Ars*. Certainly the saints deserve the most brilliant biographers they can get; and a great literary man, when he writes about them, will carry their appreciation to minds that otherwise would be closed against them. Still, we do not like to see them overwhelmed by the grandeur of their biographers. In short, the biography ought to fill us with enthusiasm for its subject rather than for its author.

Perhaps it was the sheer simplicity of Boswell that enabled him to score his triumph. He set out to tell us all about Johnson — to give us a book about Johnson — to advertise Johnson and not Boswell, and the result is a masterpiece. "Boswell's *Life of Johnson*," Macaulay wrote, "is assuredly a great, a very great work. He is the first of biographers. Many of the greatest men that ever lived have written biography. Boswell was one of the smallest men that ever lived, and he has beaten them all."

At any rate, it is agreed that some of the saints have not been fortunate in their biographers; and this is a fault that we readily pardon when we remember how difficult the art of biography is and how few have succeeded in it.

Biography ought not to be, although it frequently has been, a mere enumeration of events. If it confines itself to the undertakings and projects of its subject, it may satisfy the demands of history and be excellent as a chronological table; but it will not be a *life*. The *Acta Sanctorum* are not always the lives of the saints. It is Plutarch, himself a great biographer, who reminds us that it is not their exploits which reveal the virtues of men but their sayings, their jests, their private behavior, their domestic relations, and so on. A mere anecdote, a piece of small gossip, may throw more light upon the character of a great man than the most imposing historical monument. Thus, Fr. Faber said, "It is not always what we read of in the lives of the saints that made them saints, but what we do not read there."

What is certain is that when we do get a really good biography, the saint, by its means, enters once for all into our understanding and into our heart. There is no doubt, for example, about the English life of St. Robert Bellarmine. It is as interesting as an Eastern tale; it quite definitely and finally settles the question of the saint's greatness, goodness, amiability, humanity, and all-around excellence and attractiveness; and you feel, when you have read it, that St. Robert is now safe as far as English readers are concerned. So, too, with Cardinal Capacelatro's life of St. Philip Neri. Here is a study, not of the biographer's literary style, but of the career and, above all, the character of St. Philip; and it is to St. Philip that the admiration of the reader is directed.

In some few cases, the saints wrote their own biography, and, by so doing, they not only saved us a great deal of trouble, but they took the short road to our hearts. Out of his *Confessions*, St. Augustine emerges as a figure of real flesh and blood. St. Thérèse's exquisite *Histoire d'une âme* has been translated into every European tongue and into several languages of the East. Probably millions who never knew or even suspected what a saint was really like, now, thanks to this simple story, do know and are all the better for knowing.

After all, what do we know, what can we know, of the inner life of human beings except what they choose to tell us? "No man knoweth the things of a man, but the spirit of the man which is in him." And, of course, some men are more difficult to understand than others. Newman was a difficult man to understand. "J.H.N. is a queer man," wrote one of his friends. "Who can understand him?" wrote another. Certainly, without the *Apologia*, he would not have been understood at all.

The autobiography, indeed, is as valuable as the real photograph of a dead person that we are lucky enough to possess, and the biography resembles an attempt to reproduce the portrait from a death-mask. But, of course, the autobiography must be sincere. Rousseau and Goethe wrote autobiographies; but as you read, you feel somehow that they are relating only what they want you to know. They rather remind us of the non-Catholic lady who said of her confessor, "Of course, I don't tell him everything."

And failing an autobiography, there is nothing like letters. "In letters," writes Cardinal Bourne, "we see the character. Motives, hesitations, doubts, worries, perplexities — often so wonderfully like our own — stand forth, and the person takes before our eyes a distinctness such as mere biography fails to depict."

From history we learn all about the achievements of St. Basil; but without his letters, we would know very little about the man. History explains why he is one of the greatest Fathers of the Church; but the letters explain why he is, at the same time, one of the most attractive.

From history it is extremely difficult to form in the mind a correct picture of St. Jerome. On the troubled horizon that encircles his period, he appears altogether rugged and warlike. When we look into the volume of his correspondence, we find a gentle and kindly man; a man of heart; a man of strong affections and generous attachments; a man playful and humorous and with a remarkable fondness for children.

In his letters as in his sermons, St. Bernard reveals the extraordinary warmth and tenderness of his nature. In those of St.

Augustine, we get an insight into the simplicity of this great man. For example, to his friend Profuturus he speaks freely of his aches and pains and confides the nature of his humiliating infirmities. One of his letters to St. Melania and her daughter-in-law Albina, starts off as follows: "Although from the state of my health or from my natural constitution, I cannot endure cold, still I have never had a chance of suffering greater feverishness than I have done during this dreadful winter, because of my inability — I shall not say to go, but to fly to you now that you are settled so near. Indeed, to see you I would have flown across the seas."

The correspondence of St. Madeleine Sophie exhibits the real woman — shrewd, strong-minded, warm-hearted, with an opinion and humor of her own. So, too, the few letters of St. Bernadette that are to be found in her biography are a revelation of the culture and refinement that sanctity brought to her soul. Considering what she had been, her poverty and backwardness, it is astonishing to find her writing to her friends and relations with so much gracefulness and depth of feeling, combined with a sound and practical common sense.

Like ourselves, some of the saints detested letter-writing, and others again enjoyed it thoroughly. St. Leonard of Port Maurice corresponded with kings and titled people, but a complaint was made against him that he wrote his letters (even those to his friend the Duchess of Strozzi) on odd scraps of paper salvaged from the wastebasket.

Mary Ward[7] from her prison wrote constantly to her spiritual daughters. Her letters were written on rough pieces of paper and

---

[7] Mary Ward (1585-1645) entered the Poor Clares as a lay sister, but later founded a community of women dedicated to active work in the Church.

written with lemon juice, a trick she had acquired in England owing to the Penal Laws. Mary Ward is not a canonized saint, but she was a very saintly person; so that we have at least one saintly person who actually made use of invisible ink. These unique letters are still in existence and are among the treasures of her Institute.

St. Teresa of Avila loved to send and to receive letters, and she took particular pains over her own. She is in fact the Madame de Sévigné[8] of the saints, and she would have endorsed every word of what Lacordaire said of letter-writing: "It is a very pleasing thing to write to those one loves; and if life was intended simply for the enjoyment of lawful pleasures, we should never tire, near or far, of conversing with those souls whose life forms part of our own."

Indeed, in days gone by and especially in those times that we call the Ages of Faith, letter-writing was cultivated as a real art and by none more so than by those who were shut up in cloisters, trying hard to become saints. This was the one great consolation they allowed themselves. Elsewhere we have spoken of the "formulas" used in the monastic letter-writing of the past. The most oft-recurring of these formulas is a demand for a speedy reply. "To —, I adjure thee, by thy gentleness, visit us often by letters; that the long distance which separates us may not triumph over those who are united by the love of Christ." Lioba says in one of her letters to St. Boniface, "I ask thee, too, deign to correct the homely style of this letter, and to send me for a model some words of thine which I crave eagerly to hear." And again, Egburga writes to him, "Deign to send me for my comfort a few words from thy hand, that in them I may always have thee with me." Indeed, we come across many traces of the same anxiety in the letters of St. Augustine himself.

---

[8] Madame de Sévigné (1626-1696), granddaughter of St. Jane Frances de Chantal, noted for her letter-writing.

He writes to St. Jerome, "I beg you not to disdain to reply to me, even if it be only occasionally."

It is very charming to think of that courteous and affectionate communication carried from one end of the Continent to the other. At a time when the apostolate of the pen was impracticable, these religious men and women, separated by long distances from home and country, employed the pen in the interests of fraternal charity and mutual consolation. How busy the couriers must have been carrying the correspondence of the Irish monks from France, from Italy, from Switzerland, from the Rhine, and even from Iceland, to their superiors and brethren at Bangor and Cork and Clonmacnoise! What news they had, they sent, and always they demanded news in return; and they were no doubt as eager for tidings of their loved ones as was St. Bernadette and as are we ourselves.

Chapter Five

The Joy of the Saints

St. Francis of Assisi bade his followers leave sadness to the Devil. St. Leonard of Port Maurice did not go quite so far. "Leave sadness," he said, "to those in the world. We who work for God should be lighthearted."

The poor world must be rather annoyed at receiving a legacy of this sort. Certainly, worldly people would be very astonished to hear sadness described as their perquisite and monopoly. In its own obstinate way, the world persists in associating the fervent practice of religion with the features and furniture of the undertaker.

"Surely religion was never meant to make people miserable!" This is the sort of half-question that is put to us over and over again; and, like the man who was asked if he had stopped beating his wife, we hesitate between yes and no. To cast us down in order to raise us up is certainly one of the functions of religion. And apart from this, there will, no doubt, always be those who insist upon making themselves unhappy about religion.

Religion, like every other blessing, must be approached in the right spirit and handled in the right way. But since, as St. Thomas says, "happiness is the natural life of man"; and since religion is intended to enrich our natural life and not to impoverish it ("I am come that you may have life and may have it *more abundantly*"[9]), it follows, because it must follow, that religion aims at expanding and not suppressing the *joie de vivre* that is in us.

St. Madeleine Sophie wrote in one of her letters, "If the world knew our happiness, it would, out of sheer envy, invade our retreats; and the times of the Fathers of the Desert would return when the solitudes were more populous than the cities."

"It is always springtime in the heart that loves God," the Curé of Ars declared; and he spoke from experience. St. Philip Neri also insisted on this. At table, on a feast day, he started a discussion on joy. Each guest had to give an opinion. "No doubt," the saint playfully observed, "Baronio will tell us that Christian gladness springs from constant meditation on death." His own opinion, however, was this: "Christian joy is a gift of God flowing from a good conscience."

"The soul of one who serves God," said St. John of the Cross, "always swims in joy, always keeps holiday, and is always in a mood for singing."

The tidings of our religion are "tidings of great joy."[10] "Your hearts shall rejoice," our Lord said, "and your joy no man shall take from you."[11] Doubtless the Holy Spirit still dwells in His Church, and joy is one of His gifts. He is the inspiration of all holy lives; sanctity can be learned only in His school; and therefore joy is one of the notes of sanctity. "A saint who is sad is indeed a sad sort of saint." In Holy Scripture, it is the just man who is told to "feast and

[9] John 10:10.
[10] Luke 2:10.
[11] John 16:22.

rejoice before God and be delighted with gladness."[12] "Be glad in the Lord, ye just; and glory all ye right of heart."[13]

"Laugh and grow strong" is one of the sayings of St. Ignatius. "I see you are always laughing," he says to Francis Coster. "I am glad of it; and while you are faithful to your rule, you cannot be too merry."

St. Teresa, as we have seen, prayed to be delivered from "sour-faced saints."

"I will have no sadness amid the thorns of life," St. Catherine of Ricci said, "but only manly patience."

"I will have no sadness in my house," St. Philip Neri declared, and he kept his word, for we are told, "Philip's room is not a room but a paradise."

"He was as great an enemy of sadness and trouble as he was a friend of peace and joy": thus the Bishop of Belley writes of St. Francis de Sales.

In the very best sense, the saints made the most of both worlds. "He was one of the happiest men that ever I met," is Erasmus's description of St. Thomas More. "Let nothing affright thee," is the motto recommended by St. Teresa. We do not find the saints snarling at life or indulging in "sullenness against nature." They did not indeed shut their eyes to the evils of our existence here below. They accepted life as they found it, without expecting to get from it either more than it could give or less. Defective they knew it to be, but they believed that something could be done to make it better and happier; and that *something* they tried their best to do. The poisonous weed of pessimism has never taken root in Catholic soil.

[12] Ps. 67:4 (RSV = Ps. 68:3).
[13] Ps. 31:11 (RSV = Ps. 32:11).

The solitaries certainly interpreted the evangelical precepts very strictly, and they made very heroic efforts to put them in practice. "Go sell what thou hast and give it to the poor and follow me":[14] this text sent thousands of them into the desert. But it is related of St. Anthony, their patriarch, that devout pilgrims flocked out in crowds and sought his cell in order to look at his face, which, in the extremity of old age, reflected the joy and gladness of his soul.

St. Francis gave a very literal interpretation to the text "Call no one father but God";[15] yet it has been said that the sun has never really shone over Assisi since he died. He apparently infected the very air with the spirit of joy, and the echoes of his singing still resound in the hills and valleys of Umbria.

"I have learnt the lesson of unbelief," Goethe lamented. "I have lost faith in the world." But the saints never lost faith even in this world. St. Vincent de Paul approached more closely than most men to the sordid and seamy side of life; and yet the very sight of his face "always made the beholder happy"; and the last word that he ever spoke, *confido*, is the watchword of an optimist. St. Dominic's life's work was to fight the battle of faith against those who had lost faith; but he never lost faith even in human nature. An early life of him says that "his face was always joyous, and people ran after him as he walked through the street."

Even death, that most terrifying thing in human experience, could not shake the confidence and serenity of the saints. By another curious paradox, death is commonly most feared by those who steadily refuse to entertain the thought of it. Dr. Johnson, strong-minded man though he was, found the prospect terrifying.

[14]Cf. Matt. 19:21; Mark 10:21; Luke 18:22.
[15]Cf. Matt. 23:9.

"The whole of life," he maintained, "is but keeping away the thoughts of death." Perhaps this was his mistake. Skulls as table decorations we certainly do not relish at all, but they may have served a more practical purpose than we think. At any rate, the undeniable fact remains that the saints who constantly lived in the presence of death feared it not at all.

"The perfect love of God," said St. John of the Cross, "makes death welcome and most sweet to the soul." When the Poor Clares of Amiens, who were in hiding during the French Revolution, were caught and thrown into prison, Sr. St. Joseph said, "Hurrah, we shall all go straight to Paradise!" They were not guillotined, however, no doubt greatly to Sr. St. Joseph's disappointment.

"I suffer much, but I am in an astonishing peace. I am full of confidence": this was how the Little Flower talked on her deathbed.

Br. Elias rebuked St. Francis of Assisi for singing on his deathbed. "He ought rather to be thinking of death," he said. But, of course, that is exactly what he was doing, and so he sang. Did not the Carmelite martyrs of Compiègne sing the Litany of Loreto on the scaffold?

The Poor Man of Assisi had nothing of this world to leave behind him, but he did bequeath to his followers the spirit of joy. He wished them to be the Troubadours of God. One of their number, Jacopone da Todi, went further and became God's Jester. Since something of the real portrait is found in every caricature, it may be that the irreverent legend of the "Jolly Friar" is based upon the gaiety and lightheartedness of St. Francis and his first disciples.

The saints knew that, in order to be permanent, efforts must be joyful; that without great courage and an unshaken confidence, we shall find it very difficult to persevere. "A glad spirit," St. Philip used to say, "attains to perfection more quickly than any other." "Anxiety and bitterness," wrote St. Francis de Sales, "are the ruin of devotion." And here is St. Clare: "Melancholy is the poison of devotion. When one is in tribulation, it is necessary to be happier and merrier because one is nearer to God."

The Cylinder of Nabonidus,[16] the father of Belshazzar, which dates from the year 555 B.C., has at least one very Christian sentiment expressed in the form of a prayer: "Give me, O God, a great joy in order that I may serve Thee the better."

It is because our Lord demands great sacrifices from His servants that He compensates and fortifies them with the spirit of joy. The measure of our joy is the measure of our generosity. The founders of the great religious orders gave a variety of shapes to the institutions they established; but they were all at one in asserting that melancholy must be banished from the cloister. St. John Chrysostom, the earliest biographer the monks had, said of them, "They have no sadness. They wage war on the Devil as though they were amusing themselves" (or, as the original expresses it, "as though they were performing a dance").

Perhaps we are inclined to take the Devil too seriously. "What is all this talk I hear about the Devil?" St. Teresa of Avila used to say. "He flies from a drop of holy water," said St. Francis de Sales. And Teresa Higginson[17] maintained that "the Devil just wants to be noticed. It is best to pay as little attention to him as possible."

St. Anselm said of the monks of his day, "They fill the world with their songs of joy." Yet the foolish world will have it that melancholy is the royal road that leads to the cloister. True, there is one saint whom disappointment in love drove to a convent. St.

---

[16]The clay Cylinder of Nabonidus was discovered in the Temple of Shamash at Sippar and records in cuneiform the reconstruction by Nabonidus of the temples of the moon-god and the sun-god.

[17]Teresa Higginson (1844-1905) English schoolteacher who promoted devotion to the Sacred Head of Jesus.

Hyacintha of Mariscotti was no doubt meant to be the exception that proves the rule.

What charming and delightful names those religious gave to the places where they built their monasteries: "The Bright Place," "The Happy Meadow," "The Gate of Heaven." There was one in Spain near Burgos that was called "The Delights" and one in France called "The Bird's Nest." Two Abbeys bore the name "Joy." A Cistercian monastery in Nivernais was called "Consolation," and our own Netley was "Joyous Place." And the people who inhabited these places were so delighted with them that they often reproached themselves for it.

When Alcuin left his cloister to go to the court of Charlemagne, he addressed to it a very touching farewell: "O my cell, I shall never see thee more. I shall see no more the woods that surround thee nor the gardens where the lily mingles with the rose. I shall hear no more the birds who, like ourselves, sing Matins in praise of their Creator." And he adds, "It is Thou, O Christ, and Thy love which has filled our hearts and made them glad — Thou, our glory, our life, our salvation."

Chapter Six

The Health of the Saints

With all their austerities, the saints were well aware that the body is the servant of the soul, and that a master who has no care of his servant is sure to be badly served. "Take care of the body," St. Teresa writes to one of her nuns, "because it must serve the soul." To fight even spiritual battles, we require physical strength. Those who went to the greatest extremes in their effort to keep their passions down, knew that "the cooperation of the body must be enlisted in the struggle against the body." It is true that St. Teresa insists that "it is a mistake to imagine that one requires to be in good health in order to be able to pray," but she only meant — what, indeed, she says — that prayer is not so much a question of strength as of love and of custom.

St. Ignatius thus wrote to St. Francis Borgia, "You should not weaken your bodily nature because the spiritual cannot act with the same energy. We ought to love the body and wish it well, when it obeys and assists the soul." St. John Fisher nerved himself for his great trial by fortifying his body. On the morning of his execution, he paid particular attention to himself, much to the astonishment of the Lieutenant of the Tower. "I will not hinder my health one minute of an hour," the martyr said, "but I shall prolong the same as long as I can by all reasonable means." St. Philip Neri quite approved of his niece's praying to get better: "Because we can do a great many things in health that we cannot do in sickness."

It is, of course, quite possible to discover in the life of this or that saint conduct that looks very much like imprudence. Real imprudence it may have been. They were human beings, all of them, and even the greatest among them did not always act prudently. Besides, they were not overly interested in themselves, and this very disengagement from self may lead to imprudence. Absorption in any pursuit almost inevitably implies a certain amount of self-neglect. Indeed, we find the saints acknowledging their imprudence quite frankly.

St. Ignatius admitted that in his early days at Manresa, he had carried penance too far. He regretted to find his strength and efficiency impaired by the rigors of his first fervor.

St. Francis of Assisi confessed, at the end, that he had been too hard on poor Brother Ass.[18] Certainly, he was far from recommending to his Brethren the austerities he practiced himself. He insisted on their exercising consideration and common sense where their health was concerned. "We must give Brother Body no right to murmur, saying 'I can't stand upright and attend to prayer nor be cheerful, for thou dost not satisfy my needs.' "

The same change of mind is seen in St. Jerome. "The immoderate long fasts of many," he writes, "displease me; for I have learnt by experience that the Ass that is too much fatigued on the road seeks rest at any cost. In a long journey, strength must be supported."

Therefore, the indiscretions of the saints must be judged for what they were — namely, indiscretions. Generous as God's grace

---

[18]Brother Ass was St. Francis's name for his body.

made them and ardent and impetuous as some of them were by nature, they felt called upon to give themselves and to sacrifice themselves even to imprudence. Frederick Ozanam was a very holy man. He never spared himself, and he died at quite an early age. Lacordaire wrote of him: "What a difference if, instead of forcing life as Ozanam did, he had slept eight hours a day and worked but six. He would still be alive. He would still have thirty years before him — that is to say, six hours' work multiplied by three hundred sixty-five and then by thirty."

But, after all, the servants of God have no monopoly of these indiscretions. The servants of the world also sacrifice health and ease and peace of mind and bodily comfort in the interests of ambition, fame, wealth, or passion; sometimes even in the interests of next to nothing at all. One of the Greek philosophers put out his own eyes in the interests of philosophical meditation, and Empedocles committed suicide in the interests of sheer vanity. These are scandalous extremes, but we find scientists and doctors risking and losing their lives in the interests of research. The discovery of the lightning conductor nearly proved fatal to Benjamin Franklin, and the discovery of nitrous oxide nearly proved fatal to Humphry Davy. Edison at one period of his career worked for twenty hours a day; and Michelangelo often labored in his studio for a week without taking off his clothes. What strains and hardships will not businessmen impose upon themselves! They will rise early and retire late, and protest that they have no time to be ill or to take a holiday: "They indeed, that they may receive a corruptible crown, but we an incorruptible one,"[19] as one of the saints says.

One hears a great deal nowadays of the merits of "living dangerously," but it is an old theory reappearing in a new form of

[19] 1 Cor. 9:25.

words. *"L'audace, l'audace, et toujours l'audace"* ("Boldness, and again boldness, and always boldness"), Danton expressed it many years ago. *"Audaces fortuna juvat"* ("Fortune favors the bold"), the pagans expressed it long before Danton. The same sentiment underlies the proverb "None but the brave deserve the fair." "Safety first" is felt to be a contemptible principle except in the busy streets. And certainly, the saints did not play for safety. Had they done so, there would be none of them. There would be no St. Vincent de Paul, no Father Damien, no martyrs, no confessors; and St. Peter would never have jumped into the sea. If they made heavy demands upon the body, this shows that, at any rate, they had great faith in the body and paid it the handsome compliment of believing it to be capable of great things.

And with all their rigors and self-denial, they did not do so badly. St. Anthony the Hermit died at the age of 104 with all his teeth in his head. Vice and excessive self-indulgence have probably impaired more constitutions and shortened more lives than ever virtue and sanctity did. Fasting and abstinence have been called "the cure of St. Charles Borromeo" — and with literal truth. He did for himself by fasting and abstinence what no doctor was able to do for him: he cured himself of a very vexatious malady that Alban Butler calls "the phlegm"; and naturally he passed on the good news to others. Being a saint, he did not patent the cure or try to keep it to himself. For example, Lewis Cornaro was cured of a complication of diseases that threatened his life at the age of forty; and, thanks to "the cure of St. Charles Borromeo," he lived to be 100 and to write a book describing his case.

The saints have a very fine record for longevity. There are a dozen centenarians among even the best known of them. St. Romuald, a strict and ascetical Camaldolese, holds the record of 120 years. St. Eusignius was 110, and he was martyred. St. Anthony the Abbot was 105. St. Nilus and St. Paul the Hermit and St. Lupus of Troyes covered 286 years between them. Some of the saints most tried by ill health lived to a great age. St. Alphonsus was eighty-nine; St. Alonzo was eighty-six; St. Philip Neri was eighty; St. Joseph Calasanctius was ninety-two; St. Albert the Great was eighty-eight; St. Robert Bellarmine was seventy-nine; St. Madeleine Sophie was eighty-four. Of the more modern saints, St. Vincent de Paul, was perhaps the healthiest and most robust. He was eighty-five when he died.

And when we read accounts of the extreme privations of the earlier saints, we must have in mind the all-around hardihood of the ages in which they lived. In comparison with ours, the bodies of our ancestors were made of cast iron. It makes one shiver even to think of the medieval castle with its massive walls, lack of glass windows, stone floors and enormous draughty apartments. Yet, there are grounds for believing that even wealthy people at that time wore no nightclothes at all. Highland Chieftains used to sleep on the moors in the depth of winter with no extra covering except the plaid. Scott tells us of one who sharply rebuked the effeminacy of his son in making a snowball to serve as a pillow.

It does not in the least follow that what we consider austerities would have been considered such in the early church or even two or three hundred years ago. Then, "East is East, and West is West." The Fathers of the Desert lived in the East, where overeating is a physical impossibility. Thus we find the monks of St. Martin pleading for a relaxation of the primitive Rule on very practical grounds: "We are Gauls, and it is inhuman to compel us to live like angels." They had at any rate one great saint on their side here, for it was St. Athanasius who called fasting "the diet of angels." So, too, St. Benedict recognized that allowances must be made not only for changed places but for changed times. In his Rule, he says,

"Although we read that wine is not a drink for monks at all, yet since in our days they cannot be persuaded of this, let us at least agree not to drink to satiety."

A saint is quoted as saying, "There ought to be an invalid in every religious community." This was not intended to suggest that disease is a good thing. It is by no means a good thing. What the saint meant was that the presence of sickness would bring God nearer to the house by reason of the patience and charity that would be exercised in it. Again, it is said of St. Bernard that, when he could, he insisted on founding his monasteries in unhealthy localities. Whatever may have been his motive for this, at any rate the unhealthy localities did not remain unhealthy for very long. In fact, the monks have been accused of getting hold of the most beautiful and most salubrious sites.

The saints did not pamper themselves; but still, in accordance with the recognized ideas of their day, they tried to do their duty to the body. St. Augustine's Rule is very explicit on this matter. He allows fasting only as far as the health permits. He tells his nuns that after any illness, they must build up their strength. He warns the superiors that if any Sister should complain, she must be believed, and if there is any uncertainty, the doctor must be consulted.

"Let everything be done with moderation," the Rule of St. Benedict says. "Everyone hath his proper gift from God, one thus, another thus. For this reason, the amount of other people's food cannot be determined without some misgiving. Let the weakness of the old and the very young be always taken into account, and let the full rigor of the Rule as regards food be in no wise maintained in their regard. Let the weaker be helped so that they may not do their work in sadness. Let one be chosen as cellarer[20] who is

[20]The person in charge of provisions.

wise, and let him not make the Brethren sad. What is given, let it be given so that no one be troubled or distressed. Let two of the Brethren who can perform their duties well be given charge of the kitchen."

St. Teresa wrote to one of her nuns, "Do not allow the Prioress to leave off eating meat. Make her take care of her health." To Bl. Agnes of Bohemia, St. Clare gives the same prudent advice: "As your flesh is not iron, nor have we the strength of marble, I beg you to avoid a too rigid abstinence, so that you may render our Lord a service full of reason and seasoned with the salt of prudence." St. Vincent de Paul writes to Louise Marillac, "Take care of your health, and honor our Lord's cheerfulness."

St. Philip Neri may be almost said to have put fasting in its place. To those who were forever talking about it, he said, "All the holiness of a man lies here [pointing to his forehead] within the breadth of two fingers." And to the Dominican novices whose picnics he used to join, he would say, "Eat away, my sons. It makes me fat to see you eat."

When the monks complained to their abbot that St. Dositheus never fasted, the abbot answered, "He does not fast, but he never gives way to his self-will." And St. Albert the Great maintained that one tear shed over our Lord's Passion was worth more than a year's fasting.

The Pharisees were certainly great fasters, and no set of men gave our Lord so much trouble and annoyance. The one in the parable boasted that he fasted twice in the week — and yet he was not justified.[21] When they reproached the disciples of John the Baptist with not fasting, our Lord took the disciples' part;[22] and

[21] Luke 18:10-14.
[22] Matt. 9:14-15; Mark 2:18-19; Luke 5:33-34.

over and over again He made it plain that fasting was quite compatible with hypocrisy and pride.[23] As a great saint said, "Fasting is good, but humility is better."

That the saints valued good health we can gather from the care and the attention they lavished upon the sick. To no aspect of the law of charity did they attach greater importance. "By neglecting the sick," said St. Teresa, "we incur a terrible responsibility." "Before all things, and above all things," the Rule of St. Benedict enjoins, "special care must be taken of the sick so that in very deed they be looked after as though it were Christ Himself whom we served."

Popular devotion has associated individual saints with certain diseases — made them, so to speak, the patrons of those diseases, the special protectors of those who suffer from or are threatened with them. Erysipelas used to be called St. Anthony's Fire, and chorea is still called St. Vitus's Dance. St. Catherine of Alexandria is invoked against diseases of the tongue; St. Apollonia against the toothache; St. Blaise against diseases of the throat; and St. Stanislaus against palpitation of the heart. St. Galla, St. Aldegunde, and St. Peregrine are commonly believed to have some power in protecting us from the scourge of cancer; and people who suffer from headaches are usually advised to pray to St. Teresa of Avila, who was a martyr to that complaint. St. Servulus is the patron of the paralyzed and St. Dymphna of the insane.

Again, it is significant how prominently doctors figure in the calendar of saints. St. Luke, St. Cosmas, St. Damian, St. Pantaleon, and St. Philip Benizi are a few of the names that come to mind, but the beautiful prayer composed in the seventeenth century by the head of the Paris Faculty of Medicine for the use of the Catholic

---

[23] For example, Matt. 6:16.

Doctors in that city, begins by invoking "all the saints who excelled in the practice of medicine and in the exercise of healing charity (*therapeutica caritate*)"; then it salutes fourteen of them by name. In the *Notices sur les Saints Médecins* by the Benedictine Père Fournier (himself a doctor), details are given of some seventy saints who practiced medicine, of whom five are women: St. Zenais, St. Leonilla, St. Hildegarde, St. Sophia, and St. Nicerate. From the very beginning, the Church held the medical profession in the highest possible esteem, associating its work with her own and teaching its members to make it a real apostolate. Indeed, it would be difficult to exaggerate the debt that medical science owes to the Church. For centuries, the study of medicine was almost confined to the clergy.

The saints who have written on the subject — for example, St. Augustine in his letter to Proba — are emphatic that to neglect the ordinary remedies prescribed by medical men is to transgress the law of that charity which everyone owes to himself. Christian science would have had short shrift at the hands of even the great ascetics. St. Charles Borromeo and St. Alphonsus were most docile to their doctors' advice. Indeed, God Himself directed Isaiah to apply dry figs to the abscess from which Hezekiah was suffering.[24]

The saints did the best they could for themselves and made the most of the health, good or bad, that was granted to them; and that is about all that anyone can do. They tried to avoid two extremes equally dangerous: preoccupation with health and recklessness regarding it. If they erred at all, it was certainly in the direction of the second extreme. The harpist does not want to make his strings either too slack or too tight. If they are too slack, there will be no music; and if they are too tight, they will probably

[24]Cf. Isa. 38:21.

break. But if there is to be a mistake at all, the harpist will have the strings rather too tight than too slack. Certainly, an age like ours, in which speed and excitement and artificial food do so much to impair people's health, has very little cause to criticize the imprudences of the saints or to accuse sanctity of being unhygienic.

It is not always the giants who do most; that is certain. "My health is very bad," St. Teresa wrote, "but God does so much through me that I laugh at myself sometimes." The biographies of the saints — and indeed the biographies of most illustrious men — exhibit the spectacle of men and women sorely tried by infirmities, and yet carrying out tremendous undertakings. Most great people have been rather delicate people. St. Alphonsus made a vow never to waste a moment of time, and he kept it in spite of the fact that he received the Last Sacrament nine times, was constantly ailing, and for thirty years was partially paralyzed. St. Philip Neri was full of labors although he was weak and regularly subject to Roman fever. St. Hugh of Lincoln had the energy of a strong man, yet he was a martyr to headaches. Bl. Julie Billiart was a cripple, and St. Spes was blind. And it was a saint — and an inspired one — who said, "The weak things of this world hath God chosen that He may confound the strong."[25]

---

[25] 1 Cor. 1:27.

Chapter Seven

The Saints and Animals

"Wholly wrapped up in the love of God, the Blessed Francis did perfectly discern His goodness not only in his own soul but also in every creature whatsoever, by reason whereof he was affected with a singular and overflowing love towards creatures." This is how the *Mirror of Perfection* writes of St. Francis of Assisi. Perhaps no saint, or at any rate, none that we know of, ever rejoiced so tumultuously in the poetry of nature. He composed a "Canticle of the Creatures" and sang it all over the place. He talked and preached to the birds, as St. Anthony did to the fish; but alone among the saints he tried to be "kind" to creatures like fire and water. He carried family pride and the claims of lineage further than they have ever been carried. He established a relationship with the sun and moon and stars. He called water his sister and fire his brother. Such is the culture of great sanctity.

The saint who only wants to be a saint becomes a great number of other things and, above all, an artist. The saint is haunted, as Fr. Faber says; that is to say, he sees what other men do not see. And his eyesight is not only strengthened, but it is refined so that he reads into all the beauties of nature a rich parable of the Divine

Beauty. Thus, to the psalmist, the firmament declared the work of God's hands,[26] and to St. Augustine the design of creation was "a voice," and earth and air and water were "images" and "a similitude." "Every creature," said St. Francis, "doth cry out and say, 'God hath made me for thee, O man.' " Very well, every creature must be loved and respected in return for its services. "To love God," said St. Gertrude, "is to love all that is of and from God."

It does not surprise us, therefore, to find in the histories of the saints endless examples of their humane and intimate dealings with animals. We feel that this is as it should be. Anything else might not scandalize us, but it would worry us. Hunting dogs, it is true, are blessed on the feast of St. Hubert, but the blessing of St. Hubert is not invoked upon the chase. St. Hubert is invoked as a protection against dog bites. He had been fond of hunting, but after his conversion, he never hunted again. He is the protector of hunters perhaps, but not of the hunt.

Participation by the clergy in hunting has been under the censure of the Church from the earliest times; and it is clear from her legislation that she regarded such a sport as alien from the gentle character of the priest. Pope Pius V vigorously protested against the Spanish bullfight; and since his time, the clergy are prohibited under severe penalties from attending it. Indeed, this legislation of the Church, combined with her symbolism and the examples of her saints, must have contributed enormously to the humanizing of man's attitude to the brute creation.

Surely all the oxen and asses of the world have gained something from the presence of the ox and the ass in the Crib. Was not St. Francis of Assisi anxious to have a law passed obliging farmers to feed them well and allow them to rest on Christmas Day?

[26] Ps. 18:2 (RSV = Ps. 19:1).

The Saints and Animals

And long before anybody dreamed of dealing gently and tenderly with the brutes, the saints were doing it. Legend says that St. Kentigern restored to life a robin that had been stoned to death; and this was in the sixth century. Hunted otters used to take refuge at the feet of St. Cuthbert; and this was in the seventh century. Swallows used to keep themselves warm in cold weather under the cloak of St. Guthlac; and this was in the eighth century. A hunted hare fled for protection to St. Anselm and sheltered itself under his horse. The horse never had a better friend than St. Thomas à Becket, and he lived eight hundred years ago. The author of the Ancren Rule says to the Sisters, "I would rather see you leprous than cruel"; and since he allowed them to keep a cat, we can suppose that he had the cat in mind.

It is well known that St. Francis of Assisi was filled to overflowing with gigantic schemes for revolutionizing the world. He believed that he would be able to stop the Crusades if he could only have a five-minute chat with the Sultan. And he had a plan for bringing comfort to all the birds in the Holy Roman Empire. His idea was that the Emperor should pass some laws forbidding the snaring of larks and obliging all mayors and corporations to have the roads strewn with crumbs at any rate on Christmas Day. At the time, this must have sounded like pure poetry; but in our own day, laws *have* been passed forbidding the snaring of larks and forbidding the caging of certain wild birds. Assisi is probably the only town in the world in which there is a regular day-to-day feeding of birds, but St. Francis's ideas have spread in all directions. A special Christmas dinner is a common feature in our own homes for worn-out horses.

The lark of which St. Francis was so fond was the crested lark. It appealed to him because it was dressed as a good religious should be dressed: it had a real friar's hood, and its feathers were the proper penitential color. Besides, its sweet song gave it an affinity with those whom St. Francis wished to be the Minstrels of God. On the evening of his death, a great flock of them wheeled over the roof of the house in which he lay and sang their goodbye to the man who had done so much for them and would have done much more if he could only have gotten at the Emperor. The birds are still fed in the marketplace of Assisi when the *Angelus* rings each day. At the sound of the bell, they fly in from all quarters guided by an instinct handed down for seven hundred years. We may be sure the crested lark is well to the fore and that he gets the very best of the pickings.

And St. Francis would not molest even the animals that molested him. He spared the very mice that tormented him night and day. He is not alone in this certainly. St. Martin of Porres was kind to the rats that gnawed the vestments. St. Francis of Paula spared the wasps; and Bl. Joseph of Anchieta spared the vipers. When the bystanders brushed the flies from the face of the dying Curé of Ars, he said, "Leave me my poor flies."

We have no call to go as far as this, nor to imitate the Mohammedans who will not molest even savage beasts; but, as St. Francis de Sales reminds us, "even this pity has a good natural source, and those who are so compassionate to animals are likely to be not otherwise to man." Cruelty is an all-around affair. The man who acts cruelly is a cruel man; and perhaps the cruelty of man has done much to make and to keep wild animals ferocious. The wolf of Gubbio did not hurt St. Francis, and the lion did not hurt St. Jerome. "All creatures," said St. Francis of Paula, "obey those who serve God with a perfect heart." These are they who, as the Scripture promised, take up serpents without being bitten by them.[27] It

---

[27]Mark 16:18.

is quite possible that one day the fierceness of all wild beasts will vanish in the presence of man who has at last learned the lesson of the saints.

Harshness with animals was a thing that St. Philip Neri could not stand. He called the Oratorian Father who crushed a lizard with his foot "a cruel man." When a bird flew in at the window of the chapel, he took good care that nobody hurt it, and having captured it, he let it fly out again. Two caged birds that he had in his cell were always allowed a spell of liberty, and when he was ill, they used to perch on his bed. Live partridges that were sent for his table he forwarded to a lady penitent with instructions that they were not to be killed. A certain dog, Capriccio by name, came with its master to see the saint. At the end of the interview, it refused to go, in spite of all the coaxing of its owner. It was therefore left with the saint and was his faithful companion for twelve years.

But the cat of St. Philip is the most remarkable animal of its kind that ever wagged a tail. It actually cooperated with him in his playful work of mortifying the pride of his followers. They worked together, so to say, in the interests of the virtue of humility; and even the early biographers speak with evident satisfaction of the privileged position of this most memorable cat.

Cats in general ought now to be able to hold up their heads. Associated with treachery, hypocrisy, and witchcraft; accused of lending its skin to the Devil; and held in abhorrence by all the early naturalists — the cat has had a reputation as bad as can be. The Ancren Rule, it is true, allowed the Sisters to keep a cat: "You shall not possess any beast, my dear Sisters, except a cat"; and the Curé of Ars had a cat; but henceforth, at any rate for all Catholic cat lovers, St. Philip Neri's cat will be *the* cat. It deserves, indeed, to be ranged alongside John Bosco's famous dog, Grigio, which acted as a kind of guardian angel, keeping him from harm and harm from him and, on one occasion, by its sagacity actually saving him from assassination.

The Bishop of Belley, in speaking of the compassion St. Francis de Sales had for animals, says, "The Church inculcates on the clergy perfect gentleness and kindness. This is why they never take part in anything involving bloodshed." He then gives some very interesting details of St. Francis's attitude toward the whole question. The saint insisted, first of all, upon the indirect duty man owes the brutes. He looked upon it as a sin to injure for the mere pleasure of doing so. "We have no right," he said, "to deprive them of the joy of existence bestowed upon them by God."

What he thought of hunting is revealed by the following incident. A gentleman, thinking to give him pleasure, brought a roebuck in his train, and he proposed to let the dogs loose upon it in the saint's presence. In disgust Francis fled to the other side of the house, while the poor animal, on being attacked by the dogs, instinctively sought the room of its benefactor. It was thereupon dispatched, but when the venison was served up, the saint would hardly touch it, and he exclaimed, "What hellish pleasure!"

He not only never did animals any harm, but he always tried to prevent them from being harmed by others; and his biographers have remarked that the animals themselves recognized his tender and compassionate nature and would, when pursued, seek his protection. When he was saying his Office, pigeons often flew for safety into his very hands.

True, these detailed examples belong to more modern times, but that may be only because modern biographers pay more attention to such matters. That such has been the general character of God's servants we know from this: that in legend and in art, a great number of them are associated with some animal or another. There is the lion of St. Jerome, the mule of St. Anthony, the wolf of St. Vitus, the stag of St. Eustace, the sheep of St. Genevieve, the lamb of St. Agnes, the serpent of St. Verdiana, the ox of St. Silvester, the horses of St. Hippolytus, the hind of St. Giles, the spider of St. Norbert, the hawk of St. Quirinus, the goose of St. Martin, the fish of St. Ulrich, the falcon of St. Bavon, the eagle of St. Prisca, the dove of St. Gregory, the doe of St. Procopius, and the bees of St. Ambrose. In some cases, the association is purely symbolic, but if a lion really was the companion of St. Jerome, we may be sure that he was devoted to it. If a wild hog regularly visited the hermitage of St. Anthony, we may be sure that he took an interest in it. The raven must have had its share of the bread that it brought to St. Paul the Hermit; and the really authentic dog that daily fetched a loaf from the baker for its master, St. Roch, had, we may be certain, a good slice of the loaf for his pains.

"I do not think much of a man's religion unless his cat and dog are all the happier for it." With due allowance for the unnecessarily sharp point that all pointed remarks have, there is a good deal of truth in the saying. Pity for animals is part of natural goodness, and consequently it is developed and intensified rather than diminished by religion. "Never blend your pleasure or your pride with sorrow of the meanest thing that feels": this is truly a Christian sentiment.

Chapter Eight

The Wit and Humor of the Saints

Someone said, "Good humor is nine-tenths of Christianity." Of course it is not, nor anything like it. This is a "smart saying" whose value lies not in the saying but in the smartness. But a sense of humor has an important part to play in the spiritual life. Fr. Benson did not hesitate to call St. Teresa's gift of humor "a divine gift." Wisdom is from above, and it is the gift of the Holy Spirit; and humor is part and parcel of wisdom. Humor is the salt of life, and to some extent it is the salt of the religious life, preserving it from decay. G. K. Chesterton says of St. Francis of Assisi, "The sense of humor *salts* all his escapades." The history of many of the heresies is largely a history of the breakdown of the sense of humor. Their aberrations and absurdities can, apart from the Devil, hardly be accounted for otherwise. "Laugh and grow *strong*," St. Ignatius said; and to one of his novices, "I see you are always laughing, and I am glad of it."

It is significant, surely, that one of the most commonsense saints was distinguished by a playful wit and a keen sense of humor. Who ever ventured to pray as St. Teresa prayed: "From silly devotions, and from sour-faced saints, good Lord, deliver us"? "May

Heaven preserve you from being a Latinist!" she writes to a nun who was rather fond of classical quotations. In her introduction to the *Interior Castle*, she observes, "So many books have been written by learned and holy men that there is nothing left for a woman to write about." When she was asked to give her opinion on a memorandum written by Senor Salcedo, this was her comment: "Senor Salcedo never stops repeating through the whole of his paper, 'as St. Paul says,' 'as the Holy Spirit says'; and then he ends by regretting that he has written nothing but nonsense. I am going to denounce him to the Inquisition."

On a certain journey she made in company with some priests and nuns, a halt was made for the siesta. They all sat together under the arch of a bridge, and she kept up their spirits by telling funny stories. She was fond of sending verses to Fr. Gratian in order to make him laugh. She invented nicknames, and very clever ones, for those with whom she had dealings. The Nuncio was "Mathusalem," the Calced Carmelites were "The Cats" and "The Owls"; and, of course, the Discalced were "The Eagles" and "The Butterflies." She herself was sometimes "Poor Angela" and sometimes "Laurentia." She has explained the motive of it all: "What would become of our little house if each one of you hid the little wit you possess?" And in another letter she writes, "We are having great joy here, but we do not get tipsy."

"What wit that man had," wrote René Bazin of the Curé of Ars. The Abbé Toccanier sympathized with him in the vexations and sufferings he endured at the hands of the Devil. "One gets used to everything — even to the Devil," said the Curé. "The *grappin* and I are almost comrades." He asked a garrulous lady if there was any month in the year in which she talked less than usual except February; and when a priest asked permission to say Mass in his church, he replied, "Father, I only regret that it is not

Christmas Day so that you might say three." "I am never kept waiting, not even at the Vatican," a great lady said to him. "Perhaps not, Madam, but nevertheless you will have to wait here." "What must I do to get to Heaven?" asked a lady of very ample proportions. "Three Lents, my daughter." A nun said to him, "People believe that you are very ignorant, Father!" "Nevertheless I shall always be able to teach you more than you will ever be able to learn." He used to say of the crinoline, which was the fashion in his day, "Our Emperor has done many fine things, but there is something he has overlooked. He should have had all doors widened by law to admit of the passage of the crinoline." And when he saw on the wall of the chateau a portrait of a lady in evening dress, he said, "One would think that she was going to the guillotine."

Cardinal Capacelatro says of St. Philip Neri, "There was one feature in his character that never fails to fascinate the young: he was always mirthful and humorous. Like all the Florentines of his time, he was noted for a vein of pleasantry." "I eat little," he said once, "because I don't want to grow fat like our friend Francesco Scarlatti." He was a vegetarian and if, when walking with his friends, a butcher's cart passed, he would say, "Thank God, I don't need any of that stuff." St. Thomas Aquinas has somewhere a good word in favor of practical joking, and as we shall see, St. Philip was greatly attracted to the practice.

As has been remarked of St. Francis of Assisi, "The sense of humor salts all his escapades." After lodging for a time at the house of Cardinal Leo, he was beaten by devils, and he declared that this was his punishment for consorting with cardinals. Legend relates that when he sought an interview with the Sultan of Egypt with the object of converting him, a trap was laid for him. The Sultan ordered a carpet covered with crosses to be spread on the floor of the tent. "If he walks on it, I shall accuse him of insulting his God;

if he does not, I shall accuse him of insulting me." Francis, of course, walked on the carpet, and on being charged with his impiety, he answered, "You must know our Lord died between two thieves who also hung on crosses. We Christians have the true Cross; but the crosses of the thieves we leave to you, and these I am not ashamed to tread on." True or not, this story proves that St. Francis was commonly credited with a very nimble wit.

There is wit and humor in the letters even of St. Jerome. He wrote to the wife of Toxotius, whose grandfather was a pagan and a priest of Jupiter, and whose conversion they were all anxious about, "I am persuaded that Jupiter himself might have been converted to Christianity if he had had such an alliance and family as yours."

Playfulness of wit is a very striking feature of our own English martyrs. Indeed, it is surprising how full the Acts of their martyrdom are of the evidences of it. Of course, St. Thomas More is conspicuous among them all, and he has rather eclipsed the others. His sense of humor never deserted him, right up to the moment of his execution. "Assist me up," he said to the Lieutenant of the Tower. "Coming down I will look after myself."

Bl. Dominic Barberi, the Passionist who received Newman into the Church and who was in all things a most mortified man, permitted a very liberal indulgence to his sense of humor. His biography records many of his witty sayings. When a certain pious lady consulted him about her nocturnal visions, he proceeded to cross-examine her about the kind and the quantity of wine she was in the habit of drinking at supper.

We have this in one of the letters of St. Madeleine Sophie: "Our Society has not been established to prove that women can become men, even though that may be less difficult in a country [France] where so many men become women."

The Wit and Humor of the Saints

In a letter to Possidius, St. Augustine discusses the propriety of married women painting their faces. He is inclined to condemn it as being a form of deceit; and he adds, "I am quite certain that even their own husbands do not want to be so taken in." And there is St. Jane Frances de Chantal. A young man whose fiancée had entered her convent to become a nun came in a great rage and gave her a good "telling off." When the stormy interview was over, St. Jane said, "I have never listened to a panegyric that gave me greater pleasure."

There is plenty of delicate humor even in the autobiography of St. Thérèse the Little Flower; and there is evidence that had little Anne de Guigné lived, she would have developed along the same lines. We are told that when she was six, she received a beautiful doll as a compensation for losing her first tooth. Of course, her brother Jacques promptly broke the doll. Anne at first was very angry, and then, pulling herself together with an effort, she said to the governess, "It is better so. I can make the sacrifice of Abraham."

Soon after his conversion St. Ignatius was imprisoned by the Inquisition and, on being examined, was accused of teaching novelties. "My Lord," he answered, "I would not have thought it had been any novelty to speak of Christ to Christians."

The same playful humor was characteristic of St. Francis de Sales. A religious complained to him that his new superior was even worse than the old. "Instead of a horse, we now have an ass." "But," said the saint, "was not Balaam well instructed by an ass?" He rebuked an acquaintance for making fun of a hunchback. "The works of God are perfect," he said. "What! Perfect, and yet deformed?" replied the acquaintance. "Yes, perhaps he is a perfect hunchback."

In conversation and even in the pulpit, he was fond of telling amusing stories. For example: "A certain woman who always made a point of contradicting her husband fell into a river and was drowned. The husband, in dragging for the body, went upstream instead of down. When the bystanders pointed out to him that the current must surely have carried it lower down, his answer was: 'Do you imagine that even her dead body could do anything except contradict me?' "

When busybodies took liberties with his good name, he would say, "I hear So-and-so has been clipping my beard for me; but still, God somehow seems to make it grow again." This reminds us of the beard of St. Thomas More, which he protected from the axe, saying, "At any rate, my beard has committed no treason."

During the preaching of the Lent at Annecy, one of the missionaries had been "letting himself go" in denunciation of the absentees. St. Francis never cared for that sort of thing, any more than he cared for long-winded sermons. "Whom was he aiming at?" he asked afterward. "He abused us for a fault that we had not committed, since we were present. Did he want us to split ourselves up into pieces to fill the seats that were empty?"

And this wit and humor of the saints is very instructive. It reminds us of what we are apt to forget, of what we sometimes do not even suspect: that there is more real joy in a saint's life than there is in all the intoxication of worldliness. All that comes from God is joyous, and holiness comes straight from Him and is, in fact, the only attribute of His that man can imitate. Piety in the saints is blended with all that is lighthearted and exhilarating. Fulbert of Chartres described the monastic spirit as a blend of "natural simplicity and angelic hilarity"; that is to say, the saints have some of the liveliness of the angels.

It has been said of religious people, with some truth, that for one who makes piety attractive, there are nine who make it repulsive. The saints, at any rate, are always good advertisements for religion. They uphold and exhibit the "bright side" of devotion and preach the lesson of the joyful service of God. Where there is a great deal of faith, there will be always a great deal of laughter. England was "Merrie England" when she was full of faith; and Chesterton maintains that the English people have not laughed heartily since the Middle Ages. Humor has been called "the fountain of reconciliation and well-being which, smiling and indulgent, contemplates the world with a kindly eye." It was the union in them of this natural gift with the supernatural gift of faith that produced the optimism of the saints.

Chapter Nine

The Friendship of the Saints

Solomon says, "A faithful friend is the medicine of life and immortality"; and he adds the significant words: "They that fear the Lord shall find him."[28] The Old Testament delights us with the story of the friendship of David and Jonathan. "Jonathan loved David as his own soul"; and David's love for Jonathan "passed the love of woman."[29]

Our Lord Himself called the Apostles His friends, and He meant His particular friends because "all things whatsoever I have heard of my Father, I have made known to *you*."[30] And it is quite evident that He loved St. John and St. Mary Magdalene with a special affection. This encouraged the saints — even the most detached of them — to seek out kindred souls to give them their confidence and their friendship. They were well aware that, although the Gospel bases perfection upon detachment of heart, it does not therefore follow that we are forbidden to love anyone

[28]Ecclus. 6:16 (RSV = Sir. 6:16).
[29]Cf. 1 Kings 18:1; 2 Kings 1:26 (RSV = 1 Sam. 18:1; 2 Sam. 1:26).
[30]John 15:15.

with an affection stronger and more sensible than that which we are obliged to entertain for all in general. "It would be singular," says Lacordaire, "if Christianity, which is founded upon the love of God and man, ended in nothing but dryness of soul toward all that is not God. Well-regulated affections are no bar to holiness. The lives of the saints are full of such affections." And, indeed, so they are. In thus attaching themselves, the saints were really following the divine law and the example of Jesus Christ. "You have not chosen me, but I have chosen you," He said.[31]

Indeed, a whole volume might be written on the friendships of the saints — friendships that were, in the best sense of the word, particular friendships. "There is not a man who has a heart more tender and more open to friendship than mine or who feels more keenly than I do the pain of separation from those I love." This is St. Francis de Sales's description of himself; and we may be sure that it could be applied to the majority of God's great servants.

How delightful to find this in the autobiography of St. Thérèse of the Infant Jesus: "When I entered Carmel, I found in the novitiate a companion about eight years older than I was. In spite of the difference of age, we became the closest friends; and to encourage an affection that gave promise of fostering virtue, we were allowed to converse together."

The *Mirror of Perfection* tells us that when St. Francis was dying, St. Clare also was very ill. "The Lady Clare, fearing she would die before him, wept most bitterly and would not be comforted, for she thought that she would not see before her departure her Comforter and Master." Now, this is a very human situation and very human language, and we can appreciate both. This is exactly how great friends feel about one another.

[31] John 15:16.

The Friendship of the Saints

St. Teresa of Avila wrote in this very strain to her friend, Don Francisco de Salcedo: "Please God you will live until I die; then I shall ask God to summon you promptly, lest I should be without you in Heaven." Even St. Augustine used to say that he did not want to go to Heaven without his flock. And what could be more engaging than the incident related in the Chronicle of the Abbey of Fontevrault: "A nun dies and later appears to one of her sisters in religion, saying, 'Understand, my love, that I am already in great peace; but I do not know how to enter Paradise without you. Therefore come quickly, so that we may go in together.'"

How intimate and devoted was the friendship of St. Basil and St. Gregory Nazianzen! How playful are the letters that passed between them! They tease one another like lighthearted schoolboys. This friendship — one of the greatest of antiquity — was destined to be disturbed if not broken, but perhaps that only shows how human it was.

Like so many of the saints, St. Augustine had the power of winning and attracting devoted followers. Perhaps no Father of the Church had so many or such enthusiastic friends. And in the letters that passed between them, we see how generously he responded to these affections. For example, he addresses Nebridius as "My sweet friend," and he writes to St. Jerome, "O that it were possible to enjoy sweet and frequent converse with you; if not by living with you at least by living near you." Of St. Jerome, Alban Butler says, "Our Holy Doctor soon gained at Rome a universal love and esteem." "What is there in that man that so attracts one to him?" the Prussian minister remarked of Pope Pius X.

St. Anselm writes to Lanfranc, "The less I can enjoy your presence, the more the desire of that pleasure burns in my soul." And to Gundulph, "All who know Gundulph and Anselm know how much love is understood by these two names."

St. Bernard thus laments the death of his friend Humbert of Clairvaux: "Flow, flow, my tears, so eager to flow. He who prevented your flowing is here no more. It is not he who is dead but I — I who now live only to die. Why, oh why, have we loved and why have we lost one another?"

St. Clare writes to St. Agnes of Assisi: "I have written the remembrance of you on the tablets of my heart, holding you dear above all others. I love you even as your Mother's own heart did love you."

St. Boniface concludes his letter to the Bishop of Worcester, "Farewell, my well-beloved."

We are told of St. Philip Neri that friendship was one of the few innocent joys of life that he permitted himself; and certainly Providence lavished friends upon him in spite of the fact that no man ever tried the patience and virtue of his friends as did he.

Indeed, it seems to have been only necessary for people to come in contact with these saints to love them. "It is a favor bestowed on me by God," wrote St. Teresa, "that my presence always gives pleasure to others." One of her earliest biographers, Ribera, said of her, "She was and she looked so amiable that everybody loved her."

Bl. Angela of Foligno had such a hold upon the affections of all who knew her, that out of pity for their feelings, she concealed the knowledge she had of her approaching death. Gallonio said of St. Philip Neri, "He hid the secret of his approaching death, lest our hearts should be crushed with sorrow."

It is well known that many of the saints were brought into close association with women — an association marked, in many cases, by a sincere and warm attachment. John Ruskin thought he saw in the buckling on of the knight's armor by a lady's hand, a symbol of the spiritual truth that "the soul's armor is never well set to the heart unless a woman's hand has braced it." This is as may be, but before Ruskin, Frederick Ozanam had remarked, "It appears that nothing great can be done in the Church without a woman having a share in it." Elsewhere he said, "The role of Christian women is like that of the guardian angels: they lead the world."

For example, there are the friendships of St. Jerome and St. Paula; of St. Augustine and St. Melania; of St. Bernard and the Duchess of Lorraine; of St. Francis and St. Clare; of St. Philip and St. Catherine of Ricci; of St. Vincent de Paul and Madame Gondi; of St. Francis de Sales and St. Jane Frances; of St. John of the Cross and St. Teresa; of St. Alphonsus and Ven. Marie Celeste; of St. Théophane Vénard and St. Thérèse of the Infant Jesus. The Curé of Ars had St. Philomena. She was in Heaven, it is true, but a "rare and mysterious affection bound him to her. She was his Beatrix, his ideal, his sweet star, his pure light." The Abbé Monnin says, "As time went on, the harmony between their hearts grew. Henceforth the saint on earth and the saint in Heaven enjoyed a sweet and intimate friendship."

This is how St. Basil writes to the wife of his friend Nectarius to console her on the death of her son: "I know what the heart of a mother is, and when I think how very kind and gentle you in particular are, I can estimate how great must be your grief at the present moment. O plague of an evil demon, how great a calamity it has had the power to inflict! O earth, that has been compelled to submit to an affliction such as this! But let us not condemn the just decision of God. Above all, spare the partner of your life: be a consolation to one another; do not make the misfortune harder for him to bear."

St. Jerome wrote to Theophilus, "The death of Paula has so completely prostrated me that until today I have translated nothing. At one blow, I lost all comfort." And he confessed that when he tried to write her panegyric, the stylus fell from his fingers. To have a saint for a friend is to have a friend indeed.

Less known is the friendship between St. Boniface and Lioba, Bugga, and Egburga — the nuns to whom so many of his letters were addressed. Great consolation certainly these letters must have brought to a lonely man toiling in a foreign country, coming as they did from the England he loved so dearly. "Would that I could deserve to have thee for a brother," Lioba writes. "No temporal vicissitudes can move my mind from its steady guardianship of thy love," writes Bugga. And Egburga writes, "Holy Father and truest friend, deign to send me for my comfort some holy relics or at least a few words from thy hand." In one of his replies to Bugga, Boniface addresses her as "dearest friend and sister in the love of Christ, to be placed before all others of thy sex."

We must bear in mind, of course, that in those days, simplicity was a practical virtue. Christians expressed their feelings and sentiments with a naiveté to which we are strangers. We neither speak nor write the sincere idiom of the past. But our forefathers in the faith were not our sort of people at all. All their literature is marked by a charming spontaneity and exuberance of expression. Into the letters that they wrote to their friends they put the same straightforward frankness they put into their poetry and their Christmas carols.

St. Boniface, for example, writes in exactly the same strain to all his friends; that is to say, he writes as few would be willing to write nowadays. Thus, to the Archbishop of York: "To a friend worthy of being embraced in the arms of love."

St. Anselm writes, "Go into the secret place of thy heart, look there at thy love for me, and thou shalt see mine for thee." And again: "The soul of my Osbern, ah! I beseech thee, give it no other place than in my bosom."

The Friendship of the Saints

It is true that this phraseology was more or less stereotyped. Formulas were drawn up by those who were good at it, and they were circulated especially among the monasteries and convents. They served as models and were copied to form the beginnings and endings of the letter. This may explain why we find in St. Jerome's letters (for example, to Rufina) almost the identical sentences found in those of St. Boniface.

We may find a little comfort in knowing that some of the saints were rather disappointed in their friends. St. Basil and St. Gregory, as we have seen, had serious misunderstandings in the end. Dona Isabel Roser was for years the staunch friend of St. Ignatius. She could not do too much for him; and, indeed, she had once actually saved his life, by dissuading him from sailing in an unseaworthy vessel that foundered on its voyage, with the loss of all hands. At one period, the saint writes to her, "I am persuaded that if I were to forget all the good that God has done me through you, His Divine Majesty would forget me also." Yet, this same good Dona Isabel's love turned to spite. She subjected St. Ignatius to a great deal of annoyance in Rome, whither she had followed him, and she ended by taking proceedings against him for embezzlement in the Ecclesiastical Courts. Needless to say, she lost her case, and she also lost her friend.

"A friend is long sought, scarcely found, and hard to keep": with this reflection, Abbess Eangyth ends one of her letters to St. Boniface; so that it appears that even the saints shared the disappointments common to plain people like ourselves. Indeed, they sometimes lavished their affections on rather an ungrateful world. The prophets of old were stoned for their pains; and the task of the reformer is proverbially a thankless task. Scant recognition came to Fr. Damien during his lifetime: his motives were suspected, and even his character was assailed. St. John Bosco was looked upon by some as a madman. St. Teresa of Avila and St. Catherine of Siena were accused of being bad women, and their very friendships were misunderstood. Some of our English martyrs were betrayed by those whom they regarded as friends; and in the early Church, it was not uncommon for wives and daughters to be denounced to execution by their own husbands and fathers. St. Margaret of Ancona bore the ill treatment of a bad husband for many years.

But if affection is unrequited, it is never thereby wasted. There is no such thing as wasted affection. "The real reward of love is found in loving." Love is its own reward. We are happier often in the affection we feel than in that which we excite; and when, by an unhappy chance, love goes out from our hearts only to be rejected, it returns again, so that to some extent, we are the gainers.

Chapter Ten

The Cheerfulness of the Saints

"True piety is cheerful as the day." This truthful line we owe, strangely enough, to one of the saddest and most melancholy of our poets: William Cowper. Since there is no doubt about the piety of the saints, there can be no doubt about their cheerfulness. St. Peter of Alcantara said of St. Teresa, "With all her sanctity, she always appeared cheerful and agreeable." Another early biography says, "Her very looks had such a charm that they soothed and rejoiced those who approached her." This is "the glad heart that maketh a cheerful countenance," of which Holy Scripture speaks.[32] Indeed we may be sure that there never was and never will be any such thing as "a depressing sort of saint." The word *melancholy* has been used in connection with St. Margaret Mary, but we know now that this has been a mistake.

Penitents many of the saints were, such as St. Mary Magdalene and St. Mary of Egypt. Into the desert they went, carrying with them the memory of their sins; and, filled with the knowledge of God's goodness to their own souls, they mortified themselves

---

[32] Cf. Prov. 15:13.

perhaps excessively. But they were well aware that our Lord said to the man in the Gospel, "Be of good heart, son; thy sins are forgiven thee."[33]

Some of them, such as St. Pachomius and St. Anthony, fled from the corruption of their age and, in caves and on the tops of mountains, sought to escape the seductions of the fallen world. But they did not forget that our Lord had said, "Have confidence; I have overcome the world."[34]

Some, such as St. Gregory the Great and St. Catherine of Siena, threw themselves into very thankless and heartbreaking tasks, but they made no mistake about the kind of Master they were serving — a Master who said to His servants: "It is I; fear not."[35] With these very words our Lord cheered the heart of St. Teresa in the midst of the slanders and vexations that tried her. "Fear not, daughter; it is I. I will not forsake thee; do not fear."

We complain of our environment, and no doubt we have some right to complain. But the environment of some of the saints was far more depressing than ours. St. Catherine of Siena lived at a time when the Church was in a most depressing condition, and yet she never lost her good spirits. St. Philip Neri was famed for a serene and sunny cheerfulness of disposition; yet his whole life was passed in the midst of the evils of the Reformation. St. Teresa herself passed through many bitter experiences and was in some ways as sorely tried as any saint we know.

And, apparently, they escaped the depression that we associate with overwork. It fatigues the mind to listen to St. Paul's account of his labors and journeyings; yet it is this same highly strung and

[33] Matt. 9:2.
[34] John 16:33.
[35] Matt. 14:27.

sorely wrought man who tells us that "God loves the cheerful giver."[36]

It is well known that the heroism of the saints was often quite unsuspected by their generation. They were adepts at the art of concealment — "as deceivers and yet true; as known and yet unknown."[37] St. Francis of Assisi possessed nothing at all; and yet he had the air and manner of a man who owned half the district — "as having nothing yet possessing all things."[38]

St. Teresa used to attribute the good opinion people had of her to her own cunning and hypocrisy. This, of course, was her humility. But, by means of this cunning, some of the saints contrived not only to be misunderstood, but to be mistaken for very ordinary people. The Curé of Ars, for example, showed an astonishing craftiness in keeping his pot of stale potatoes out of sight; when he cured the sick, he always "blamed" St. Philomena. Cardinal Capacelatro says that St. Philip Neri veiled his miracles with a jest. Certainly, he seems to have been incessantly occupied in throwing his admirers off the scent. It is related of St. Elizabeth of Hungary that when she sat at meals with her husband, the Landgrave, she concealed the fact that she was eating next to nothing, by talking with the guests, by carving the joint, by sending for the maids, by changing the plates, and by "a thousand other artifices." St. Marcian the Anchorite spent the greater part of his life dodging admiration. Indeed, in this respect, he bears off the palm, because before he died, he gave strict orders that his body was to be buried in a secret place.

The saints "did good by stealth and blushed to find it fame." They were well instructed in the school of that Divine Master who

[36] Cf. 2 Cor. 9:7.
[37] 2 Cor. 6:8.
[38] Cf. 2 Cor. 6:10.

said, "When thou dost an almsdeed, sound not a trumpet before thee; when ye pray, pray in secret; and when you fast, be not sad, but anoint thy head and wash thy face, that thou appear not to men to fast."[39] And in many cases, they led their contemporaries astray by means of their gaiety and cheerfulness.

This, indeed, will never be very difficult as long as the stupid world refuses to believe that a man who eats once a day, sleeps three hours out of the twenty-four, and wears a hair-shirt, can be a cheerful man.

The saints were filled with the cheerful spirit of God. "We have not received the spirit of bondage in fear, but the spirit of adoption whereby we cry, 'Abba (Father).' "[40] God, through the prophet Ezekiel, sternly reprimanded the false teachers of Israel because, "with lies you have made the heart of the just to mourn whom I have not made sorrowful."[41] And so, St. Vincent de Paul bade Mlle. le Gras (St. Louise Marillac), "Honor our Lord's cheerfulness." So, too, St. Francis of Assisi: "Unto the enemy, indeed, it pertains to be sorrowful, but unto us to rejoice always."

We cannot but envy the cool facility with which these saints literally sent melancholy flying to the Devil, to whom, they maintained, it properly belongs. St. Teresa was quite emphatic on the point. St. Clement Hofbauer, using the phraseology of his day, called depression "the vapors," but he added, "the vapors of Hell." "I am never sad," said Ven. Fr. Joseph Passerat, "and I thank God for it, for [sadness] is the attribute of demons." St. Philip Neri, in the plans he made for the welfare of his boys, associated merriment with the avoidance of sin.

[39] Cf. Matt. 6:2, 6, 16-18.
[40] Rom. 8:15.
[41] Ezek. 13:22.

The Cheerfulness of the Saints

And they would not tolerate a lack of good cheer in those with whom they came in contact. The *Mirror of Perfection* tells us that it irked St. Francis to see sadness in the face. Once he composed some verses and had them set to music to "cheer up" the Poor Clares.

"My sons," St. Philip Neri was fond of saying, "be cheerful. I will have no low spirits. I will have no scruples and sadness in my house." Indeed, he feared much more harm from melancholy than from merriment. He never checked the boisterousness of his young men. When people complained of the noise they made, he would say, "Let them grumble as much as they please, and you make as much noise as you please." He himself loved to watch their sports and horseplay, and when he was asked how he could put up with it, he said that he would allow them to chop firewood on his back if it would keep them out of mischief. He would make his depressed penitents sing. To a worried priest who consulted him, he said, "Come now, let us run a race," and so they did, hand in hand. Of the saint himself, one of his biographers writes, "Cheerfulness flowed from his good, simple, frank nature. We find him always sprightly and glad."

Even the strictest and most ascetical saints had their relaxations and their recreations. This is one of the rights of human nature that is not to be denied. We find St. Charles Borromeo enjoying his game of chess and St. Aloysius enjoying his game of ball. The common recreation of her nuns used to fall flat when St. Teresa was not present. We find them, in fact, going up to her cell and coaxing her to come down; and it is recorded, "She came, and we were very merry together." St. Alphonsus could not stand moroseness or frowns at recreation. "It is better," he said, "to say silly things than to be silent." St. Madeleine Sophie had occasion once to admonish a novice who was rather wanting in gravity, but she added, "Be always merry at recreation."

In their dealings with souls, they took the cheerful and optimistic way. St. Francis de Sales insisted on using honey instead of vinegar for catching his flies. "Reverence is good, but confidence is better," said St. Thomas Aquinas. "We must be more kind than just," said St. John Chrysostom, adding, "Kindness alone conciliates." "If there must be an extreme, let it always lean toward our Lord's way of acting. You will gain nothing by command," said St. Madeleine Sophie. "You will accomplish nothing against the stream," said St. Teresa. And St. Francis de Sales: "It is better to have to account for too little severity than for too much." Indeed his cheerful broadmindedness was such that one of his friends said of him, "Francis de Sales will go to Heaven, but I am not so sure of the Bishop of Geneva."

The *Mirror of Perfection* says of St. Francis of Assisi, "His highest and chiefest *study* was to maintain both outwardly and inwardly a spiritual cheerfulness." Perhaps we have not understood this sufficiently — that good cheer is a knack, an art in fact, and the result of much planning and contriving.

People say, "You are either cheerful, or you are not; and that is the end of the matter." But, of course, the same sort of people also say, "You either love, or you do not, and that is the end of that matter."

Some effort must be made to preserve cheerfulness, as to preserve friendship and love. Love commonly dies of sheer and willful neglect; we guard it with less care than we guard our trinkets and silver spoons. And although children are cheerful by nature and by accident, we adults are not. Good cheer flows through the little one like the blood through his veins; but it is far otherwise with us who have said goodbye to illusions and whose blood and veins are not what they were. Beauty may be able to look after itself, but not cheerfulness.

The Cheerfulness of the Saints

A modern book has been written on "The Conquest of Happiness." Whatever the merits or demerits of the book, there is a great deal of truth underlying its title. We have to make some effort to "cheer up." Just as we must employ a certain amount of imagination in the service of charity, so we must employ some strategy in the service of cheerfulness.

How ingenious St. Teresa was in this way: "There is no such thing as bad weather. All weather is good, because it is God's." And again: "It comforts me to hear the clock strike, for I feel that I have drawn a little nearer to God." This is, at any rate, an improvement on the philosophy of the lady of the world who, when she was told to cheer up because tomorrow was the longest day, replied, "That means that it is only six months to the shortest."

Addison tells us of the strategy of a sick man who, when he had gout, thanked God that it was not influenza; and when he had influenza, thanked God that it was not gout. When Fénelon's[42] library was burned, he thanked God that it was not the house of a poor man; and when the Irishman was told that his house was on fire, he said, "What do I care? I am only the tenant!"

We find a great deal of this commonsense philosophy in the saints. To her dejected nuns, St. Teresa would say, "Come, come; we are not yet on the rack or among the Moors." St. Paul reproved the cowardice of the Hebrews by reminding them that they had not yet resisted unto blood.[43] When Fr. Damien discovered the symptoms of leprosy on his own person, he said, "Well, at any rate, in future when I preach, instead of saying, 'My dear brethren,' I shall be able to say, 'My fellow lepers.' " When the enemies of St. Remigius set fire to his haystacks, he and his friends, on being

[42]François Fénelon (1651-1715), French bishop and author.
[43]Heb. 12:4.

notified of the fact, galloped to the place in order, if possible, to save the stacks. When they arrived, they found the fire quite out of control. "Well, at least," said the saint, "let us warm ourselves. Fire is always good."

Things may go wrong with us, but they can never go "all wrong." No trial is ever "as bad as can be." Good and bad fortune have their innings, and if we do not lose our heads over the first, we shall not lose our peace over the second. The stars go into hiding from time to time, but they are always in their place; and, sooner or later, they peep out again more welcome than ever. "Hope likes the sunshine but hides from the rain." "What can't be cured must be endured."

Perhaps if we had fewer desires, we would have fewer disappointments. If the events of life do not come up to our expectations, it may be that our expectations are at fault. "Sweet are the uses of adversity," and the value of adversity lies in this: that it dispels our illusions; opens our eyes to the realities of life; makes us realize that One alone is perfect and unchanging and that, as a saint says, "It is only in Heaven that there are no misunderstandings." Such reflections are not a blind deception or self-hypnotism; they are the ingredients of what St. Francis of Assisi called "the study" and St. Francis de Sales called "the strategy," of Christian cheerfulness.

Chapter Eleven

⁓

The Playfulness of the Saints

That a saint may be frolicsome without prejudice to his prospects of canonization was settled once for all by St. Philip Neri. Cardinal Capacelatro, speaking of his extraordinary sprightliness, says, "I know no other saint who resembles him in this respect."

St. Philip's singularity lies not in the fact that he allowed great liberty to the playfulness of his disposition, but rather in this: that he made it one of the leading principles of his school of piety. He turned playfulness into a kind of apostolate. The municipality of Rome in the year 1898 set up a tablet on the Janiculan Hill with the following inscription: "Here in the shade of this oak tree, Philip Neri, amid the merry shouts of boys, became himself a boy again — most wisely." Priest though he was and old, he would join in the sports of those boys of his. When the game of tennis or quoits was in full swing, he would withdraw to the shelter of the tree to say his prayers. If the boys called him back, he would return to the field. He even allowed his young followers to play tennis against the wall of his room; and although the occupants of the house complained of the din, he would never permit the lads to be interfered with.

All this and much more of this nature is true of St. Philip, but it is matched by what we read of in the lives of other saints. St. John Bosco also thoroughly enjoyed a game with his boys. St. Charles Borromeo was very fond of chess, and St. Aloysius played some ball game or another. Each of them, one during his game of chess and the other during his game of ball, was asked what he would do if he were suddenly told that the world was about to come to an end, and both maintained that they would go on with the game.

Of St. Ignatius it is related that being anxious to do something for the soul of a certain Doctor of Theology, he challenged him to a game of billiards, and worse still, did it for a wager: "If I win, I shall become your servant for a month; if I lose, you will undertake to do one thing for me that will be entirely to your own advantage." "Done!" The game was played; the Doctor of Theology lost, and he was put through the Spiritual Exercises for a month.

So St. Philip Neri is not by any means the only saint who was fond of games. He is the saint of playfulness because he employed it for the sanctification of his own soul and of that of his disciples. He knew that he had a reputation for sanctity and in order to discredit it, he set himself to dance like a gypsy in the streets and public squares. Sometimes he would walk through the town carrying in his hand a branch of wild broom that he would smell with tremendous gusto. He would go into the churches with his biretta cocked at a naughty angle, and wearing over his cassock an old jacket turned outside in. He would shave off only half of his beard. When Cardinals and other great people came to see him, he would skip about in a waggish fashion and laugh as though he had lost his wits. Meeting in the crowded street a mendicant friar on his rounds, he insisted on having a "pull" at one of the little barrels of wine he carried; and to the astonishment of the bystanders, he pretended to be drinking with unrestrained relish. A lady who had a great opinion of his sanctity asked him one day how long it was since he left the world. "Left the world?" he answered. "I don't know that I have left it at all." Then turning to one of his companions, he said, "Antonio, do I not still take pleasure in pretty books and poetry and novels?"

The tricks that he and St. Felix played on one another kept the whole of Rome laughing. When they met in the street, Felix would say, "Let's see what kind of a mortified man you are," and, taking a bottle from his wallet, he would make Philip drink out of it in the sight of all the people. Then it would be Philip's turn. "Come, let us see what kind of a mortified man you are," and he would put his hat on the top of the friar's hood, adding, "Be off now." Felix would go on his way followed by crowds of delighted children laughing and saying, "Look at Fra Felice with a hat on! Come and see Fra Felice with a hat on!"

St. Philip, in fact, mortified his penitents by means of practical jokes. He would send one walking through the streets with a sandwich board about his neck with something absurd written on it; another he would order to carry an unwieldy dog in his arms; but surely the most unfortunate of all was he who, at a very grand marriage feast, was called upon to sing the *Miserere* in presence of the bride and bridegroom by way of an epithalamium!

And what an amount of fun St. Philip got out of his cat; and no doubt, the cat out of him! Indeed, like Montaigne and his cat, it is not easy to decide which of the two provided the sport and which enjoyed it. When grand people came to see him, he would receive them with the cat curled up in his lap. When he went to live at Vallicella, he left his cat behind, partly, no doubt, because he knew that it would be sure to return to its old home. In that respect, the cats of the saints are no exception to the rule of their kind. But he had another motive. His biographer tells us that he would bid now one and now another of his disciples, often men of high rank or great learning, take the key and go to San Girolamo to see how the cat was, to take her some food, and to bring back word as to whether she was comfortable and contented. On their return, he would ask, even in the presence of Cardinals, "So, you have been to see my dear cat? What nice dinner did you take her? Is she well? Did she look happy? Had she a good appetite?"

Such was St. Philip Neri. In this respect certainly, he has never been surpassed, but still we find a great deal of his spirit in other saints. St. Thomas More and he would have made a rare pair. It is well known that the martyr's household resembled a nursery full of happy children, and it did so largely owing to his inveterate love of practical jokes. Indeed, he played one upon his first wife on the very day that they were married, by presenting her with some splendid-looking jewels that, however, were made of glass. She was delighted, of course, and did not learn the truth about them until long after, when, no doubt, she laughed heartily at her own expense. He played his last practical joke on the eve of his execution. Henry, we are told, was most anxious that More should recant, and he sent a courier again and again to urge him to change his mind. "Yes, I have changed my mind," said Thomas at last. The courier therefore rushed back to tell Henry. He was then told to return and find out the particulars of the change of mind. "I have changed my mind in this sense," said the martyr, "that whereas yesterday I intended being shaved before execution, I have now changed my mind and intend that my beard shall go with my head."

St. Teresa of Avila had a great deal of this quality in her temperament. Her letters abound in sportive sallies. In one, to Antonio Gayton, she inquires after his daughter: "Let me know how you found your naughty little pickle." She got great fun out of arranging a competition between the friars and the nuns. True, it was a competition to see which of them could bear the most vexations; but it was nevertheless what she called it: a real "tournament"; and no doubt they all entered wholeheartedly into the spirit of the game.

As bishop, St. Francis de Sales was compelled to begin a campaign against the abuses connected with St. Valentine's Day. Certainly he resorted to very strong measures, even invoking the aid of the civil authority; but both the gentleness and playfulness of his character are seen in the expedient that he finally hit upon in order to preserve the good name of the custom. "In future, I myself am going to provide you with Valentines," he told his people from the pulpit. And sure enough, he sent around to every family tickets bearing the names of different saints and embellished with appropriate texts from Scripture and the writings of the Fathers. These tickets had to be drawn for by lot, and the saint on the ticket became the patron for the year. No doubt the people of Annecy enjoyed their lottery immensely.

We have already seen St. Ignatius as a billiard player. There is another incident in his life that, as Francis Thompson says, "we value as much as the records of his visions and sublimities because it helps us to keep in touch with his humanity. This lofty and ascetic saint forgot to forget his own merry and cavalier youth; he danced before Ortiz [one of his penitents]; he danced as another David; he danced the old Basque national dance. Ortiz was roused and brightened; the two, one may well think, laughed heartily together. There is a charming southern atmosphere about the tale. An English saint might perhaps have sung, if an English saint chanced to be capable of singing; but perhaps no man of the North could so far have forgotten his constitutional gravity as to dance."

This happened in 1539. Ten years before, we find dancing in full swing in a convent of Poor Clares. In an account of the celebration of the Jubilee of the Abbess of Nürenberg written by one of the nuns, we read, "We conducted the Reverend Mother to the refectory, and because of the occasion, she allowed all the Sisters to sing as much as they pleased. Toward evening, we all danced, and Mother Apollonia, who has been here fifty-seven years, danced with me, and in the most sprightly manner." What the dance was we are not told — something more stately and dignified than our dances, we may be sure — but this scene would have rejoiced the heart of St. Francis of Assisi. He was fond of doing a little dancing on his own account, and although he made no provision for it in the directions he gave to his spiritual sons and daughters, singing he strongly insisted upon. And we have good reason to believe that had he been present at the Nürenberg Jubilee, he might have improvised a kind of mimic orchestra. At any rate, the *Mirror of Perfection* tells us, "Drunken with love, the Blessed Francis would at times do such like things as this: he would pick up a stick from the ground and, setting it upon his shoulder, would draw another stick athwart — the same as athwart a viol or other instrument — and, making fitting gestures, would sing in the French tongue."

Doubtless a theory of sainted playfulness made out of such scanty materials is not a very convincing theory, but we must remind ourselves once again that biographers have not always concerned themselves with the human side of their subjects. The monuments of many of the saints are like the monuments of Babylon or Egypt: very little detail survives. We have the great monoliths of the temples, and we have the massive stones of the Pyramids; but it is only after long and painstaking excavation that we light upon some strong evidences of the domestic life of those periods. When we do, as in the case of Pompeii, we are delighted.

The Playfulness of the Saints

We are delighted because we are instructed — really instructed as to the actual life led by those ancient peoples, who, after all, must have been men and women like us.

It is the straw that shows how the wind blows. And so it is with the saints. Hidden away in a footnote we often come across what amounts to a great revelation; and reading between the lines, we may discover what the lines themselves do not tell us. "If," says Cardinal Capacelatro, "we study the saints somewhat beneath the surface, then each puts on his own special form, and this form seems more human, more akin to ourselves."

Surely the "puns" of St. Augustine are some evidence of his playfulness. The conversion of England is closely connected with a pun — the pun of St. Gregory: *"Non Angli sed Angeli"* ("Not Angles but Angels") and so on.

From the letters that passed between St. Gregory Nazianzen and St. Basil we learn that at least two of the greatest and most learned Doctors of the Church were very playful men. They were very fast friends, at any rate for a time; and at the height of their attachment, St. Gregory was very anxious that St. Basil should come to live beside him. Tiberina was the place suggested. Basil goes to look at Tiberina and finds it a dull and cheerless spot and writes to say so. Thereupon Gregory replies, "There is no use blaming me for the ice and cold of Tiberina. What a clean-footed, tiptoeing, capering man you are, to be sure. The fact is, you have set up to be a dandy. Therefore, say not a word more against our mud. If you do, I will match our wading with your trading and all the other wretched things that are to be found in towns." This is the letter of a saint, and it is a very "playful" letter; its theme is the good old stand-by of all amateur debating societies, "Town versus Country."

When St. Robert Bellarmine paid his first visit to a gentleman who was a great admirer of his, he tried (he did not succeed) to play a trick upon him by pretending to be someone else. It is a small incident in the splendid career of the saint, but it is sufficient evidence of his playfulness.

Among the friends of St. Clement Hofbauer was a well-known pantheist whom he was very anxious to convert. Finding him one day confined to a sickbed, the saint pinned to the coverlet a scrap of paper on which he had written, "A piece of the divinity is ill." This is the playfulness of St. Clement.

There was a great deal of fun and frolic mingled with the simplicity of the Curé of Ars. It is well known that he countersigned the petition organized for his removal from Ars. "Now that they have my signature, there ought to be no lack of material for a conviction." The first thing he did on being made a Canon was to sell his mozetta. "I have sold it for fifty francs," he wrote to the bishop. "The price completely satisfied me." During the campaign he conducted against what he considered the improper stylishness of female fashions, he met Jeanne Lardet while walking in the village. Jeanne was wearing the very "latest thing" in collars and, we may be sure, was feeling and looking rather proud of the fact. The eagle eye of the Curé fell upon the collar. "Jeanne, will you sell me that collar? I will give you five sous for it." "But what for, Monsieur le Curé?" "For my cat."

John Bosco was as much misunderstood in his day as was the good Curé of Ars. Some very good people, in fact, were quite convinced that he was mad. Two priests, therefore, undertook to get him safely lodged under lock and key in the neighboring lunatic asylum. It would require a great deal of tact and coaxing, but they would manage it between them. It takes one priest to understand and to manage another, et cetera, et cetera. John Bosco received them very graciously, and having soon smelled a rat, he determined to nip their plan in the bud. He therefore agreed to accompany them to the carriage that was waiting outside. "After you," said he; and then when the priests had gotten in, he said to the coachman, "To the asylum," and he slammed the door. This was the playfulness of John Bosco.

Perhaps if the truth were known, there was a playful side to the characters even of the great ascetics. Sozomen, the Church historian, calls the eremitical life the peak of philosophy. But, the genuine philosopher is a very complete man whose eyes are wide open both to the serious side of life and to the funny side. Democritus was called the "laughing philosopher." He laughed a little more than the average philosopher; but every real philosopher laughs. Therefore, from time to time — at any rate, on feast days — there may have been a "certain liveliness" in the lauras and hermitages of the Thebaid; and who knows what tricks the Stylites and the Gyrovagi may have played on one another. The monk who was ordered to unpick each evening the baskets he had made during the day may have thought it a very good joke, and perhaps it was intended to be.

At any rate, there is tucked away in a corner of the lives of the Fathers of the Desert one little incident that is something in the nature of an illumination. There was, we are told, a novice who had a high reputation for virtue even among the old and experienced solitaries. One of the latter, wishing to test the patience of the young man, entered the enclosure of his cell and so utterly destroyed the garden of herbs that he had taken so much pains to lay out, that only a single plant was left standing. Meantime, the signal for the Office was sounded, and dinner followed as a matter of course. Since the old monk had not left the garden, charity demanded that he should be invited to share the repast of the young novice. "Venerable Father," he said, "sit down, and I will prepare for you a dinner consisting of the herb that fortunately you have spared me."

Among the promises God made to Zacharias was this: "I shall dwell in the midst of Jerusalem; and the city shall be full of boys and girls playing in the streets thereof."[44] According to commentators, these promises are fully verified only in the Church — in that Church which is the fruitful Mother of saints.

[44]Cf. Zach. 8:3, 5.

Chapter Twelve

⌒

The Peace of the Saints

Dr. Johnson, living in the city of London and close to one of its noisiest streets, acknowledged that he could never think of a monastery without wanting to go on his knees, or of a hermit without wishing to kiss his feet. Renan, living in the liveliest city of the world, said that he would have given everything he possessed to have been able to see St. Mary of Egypt pacing the desert in ecstasy. Johnson was a sincere Christian, but he was not a Catholic, and he would not have approved of the principle of monastic life. Renan was not even a Christian, so the supernatural aspect of St. Mary of Egypt did not appeal to him in the least.

There is evidently no doubt about the fascination of solitude. The solitary is always a very romantic person even if he is nothing else. He will excite sometimes our sympathy, sometimes our envy, but always our interest.

Perhaps in all of us there is a little of the hermit as there is of the wanderlust. Certainly it would be difficult to find a boy who has not dreamed of a desert island and envied the isolation of Robinson Crusoe. We still hear of very busy people who intend to "retire" as soon as they can; and apparently one of our modern discoveries is the discovery that it is possible even for the married to live too close to one another's lives.

The most dissipated of our poets was most eloquent in the praise of "the rapture of the lonely shore and the pleasure of the pathless woods."[45]

Certainly much has been written of the fascination of the desert. Condemned as we are to live among noisy crowds, it does us good even to read of parts of the world that are still uninhabited and of the countryside that are still peaceful and unspoiled. And is not the very thought of the old anchorites and solitaries calculated to relieve the strain upon our nerves and to rest the tired drums of our ears? Art represents St. Gertrude of Nivelles with a mouse clinging to her pastoral staff. It is an ingenious symbol of the perfect repose of a great contemplative; and some of that repose descends upon us at the very sight of the picture, and we understand what St. Teresa meant when she said that it is often the saints whose vocation is most unlike our own who do us most good.

St. Jerome's description of the hermit Bonosus somehow soothes the soul and fills us with strange longings. "Come and behold here a youth brought up to inherit abundant wealth and noble lineage and who, forsaking mother and brothers and sisters, went forth to live on an island in a rough deserted spot, alone in a solitude where nothing is heard save the roar of the ocean. There on this lonely spot he stands alone — no! I will not say alone, for he is in the company of Jesus Christ."

And so too, St. Columba's "Farewell to Arran": "Farewell, a long farewell to thee, Arran of my heart. Paradise is with thee — the garden of God is within the sound of thy bells. The angels love Arran. Each day an angel comes to thee to join in the services.

[45]Cf. Lord Byron, *Childe Harold*, Canto iv, verse 178.

Farewell, dear cell, in which I have spent such happy hours with the wind whistling through the loose stones and the sea-spray hanging on my hair."

"Fly to the cities of refuge," says St. Bonaventure, speaking of the cloister. Are there not times in our lives when we devoutly wish we could?

Besides, when the mind and heart are disturbed, we have no inclination to confide our troubles to noisy people. Shrill voices and clamorous sympathy would make us worse; but we seek the society of the quiet and the gentle, just as the fatigued eyesight turns to the soft green of the grass. We may well thank God, therefore, that there are saints for all occasions. There are some like St. Athanasius or St. Paul who act upon us like dynamite exploding us out of our lethargy and lukewarmness; but there are others like St. Anthony the Hermit and St. John the Silent, who, when everything is at war within our raging hearts, speak to us of rest and of peace.

And these contemplatives are a useful reminder to us that the active life can be carried too far. Owing to the perils that confront the Church in our time, religion with us is very largely an organized and strenuous activity. Martha is rather in the ascendant, as, of course, she has a perfect right to be, because she is a saint. But after all, Martha and Mary were sisters; and even if we are not called to the "better part," some of that "better part" there must be in our lives. As St. Augustine says, "Did not our Lord settle the question when He took Mary's part against Martha?"[46] Mere energy is not zeal.

To work very hard for religion is not necessarily to be religious. "Take heed to thyself," St. Paul wrote to Timothy.[47] Timothy was a

---

[46]Luke 10:38-42.
[47]1 Tim. 4:16.

zealous and hardworking apostle, but it is always possible for the busiest of church workers to neglect themselves. Our spiritual expenditure ought not to be in excess of our income.

Where there is no repose, no reflection, everything will be shallow, flimsy, and cheap. We all know what sort of vessels those are that make the most sound.

> *Words are like leaves and where they most abound*
> *Much fruit of sense beneath is seldom found.*[48]

The really great thinkers of the world spoke, when they did speak, with all the force and profundity of years of brooding and meditation. "Prune down thy words," is Newman's advice; and he goes on to show that it is only when we check our small feelings and impulses that they are able to accumulate into something really great and worthwhile.

Carlyle lamented that the two greatest nations in the world were going all away into mere wind and tongue. "There is far too much talking going on," he said. What would he say now? Perhaps it is just possible so to exhaust ourselves by the discussion of our problems that we have no energy left for solving them.

"Solitude," said Fr. Ravignan, "is the mother country of the strong, and silence is their prayer."

St. Jerome had the same thought: "O desert enameled with the flowers of Christ; O solitude where the stones are born of which is built the city of the Great King."

Certainly nothing really great was ever done in this world without the discipline of quiet and recollection. The noblest works, like the temple of Solomon, are brought to perfection in silence. If Dante and Shakespeare and the rest had been merry, gad-

---

[48] Alexander Pope, *Essay on Criticism*, line 309.

about fellows, shy of their own society, they would never have enriched literature as they did.

St. John Chrysostom, St. Jerome, St. Basil, and St. Gregory of Nyssa prepared themselves for their apostolate by years of solitude. How far-reaching has been the effect on the world of the great movements associated with the names of St. Benedict, St. Francis, and St. Ignatius! And it was in solitude that they were planned: in the cave at Subiaco, on the top of Mount Alvernia, and in the grotto at Manresa. Our Lord Himself prepared for His ministry in the desert:

> *There He shall first lay down the rudiments*
> *of His great warfare, ere I send Him forth*
> *to conquer sin and death.*[49]

"Silence," says Fr. Faber, "has always been the luxury of great holiness, which implies that it contains within itself something divine." Indeed, St. John tells us that it is observed even in Heaven: "There was silence in Heaven, as it were, for half an hour."[50] Silence was the constant companion of our Lord.

> *But peaceful was the night*
> *Wherein the Prince of light*
> *His reign of Peace upon the earth began.*[51]

And during His Passion, "Silence came back to Him again, just as an old habit returns at death." "Peace" was His favorite salutation. "He is our peace," says St. Paul.[52] And He blessed us with the

---

[49]John Milton, *Paradise Regained*, lines 157-159.
[50]Apoc. 8:1 (RSV = Rev. 8:1).
[51]John Milton.
[52]Eph. 2:14.

blessing of peace: "My peace I give you"; He left peace as a legacy to us: "My peace I leave you."[53]

Renan confessed that in losing the institution of monasticism, the world had lost a great school of originality. Circumstances, perhaps, do not permit too great an extension of the contemplative system, but there will always be souls destined for a life of retirement. "I am best fitted for the shade," said Cardinal Mezzofanti, which is a confession we would not have expected from the world's greatest linguist. But the characters of some people are like celery: they develop best in obscurity. They are out of joint in society; they have no small talk; a drawing-room would be their death; and they would be broken to pieces by the commotions and agitations upon which robust natures thrive.

St. Paul, the first of all the hermits, fled into the desert to escape the persecution of Decius. He lived in hiding in a cavern said to have been used by money-coiners in the days of Cleopatra. But we are told that having found by chance experience that solitude suited him down to the ground, he resolved to return no more among men. Henceforth, it was enough for him to know that there was a world and to pray for its welfare. Of other hermits — for example, of St. Anthony — it is related that the attractions of solitude suddenly dawned upon them like a kind of revelation through hearing some portion of Holy Scripture read in Church.

But the monastic system is a precious boon even to those who are not called to be monks. The world badly needs to be reminded of the value and necessity of peace and repose. The grand achievement of St. Benedict was just that. At a time when society was sick unto death of its own sheer restlessness and violence, he tranquilized it by means of the object lesson of his Order. The *Pax* of St.

[53] Cf. John 14:27.

Benedict drew attention to the grandeur of the arts of peace. So he is called not only the founder of the Benedictines, but above all the Founder of Peace: *"Ipse Fundator placidae quietis."* One of his sons, St. Bernard, said, "We are the Order of the Peaceful." And again, "We fight for God and for peace."

What a debt civilization owes to this peace of St. Benedict! And surely this hysterical world of ours might learn a profitable lesson by looking wisely instead of foolishly into his spirit! We cannot retire into the desert as did St. Anthony and St. Paul; we are not called to the cloister as were St. Gertrude and St. Teresa. We must continue to the end to occupy the busy situation allotted to us. We must come and go and be jostled and elbowed by the crowd, and listen from morning until night to the uproar of the traffic, the stridency of human voices, and the slamming of doors. But it might be a good plan to do what St. Catherine of Siena recommended — namely, to build a little cell within our own heart. "May the peace of God dwell in your hearts," is St. Paul's blessing;[54] and that is where we want it to dwell.

If the heart is at peace, all is at peace. It is very doubtful if Byron ever experienced "the rapture of the lonely shore" of which he wrote, because he carried with him always the agitations of his passions. Not all those who went into the desert found peace there. Those experiments were not all successful. St. Gregory points this out and reminds us that a soul does not dwell in true solitude unless it possesses the secret of living within itself. He eulogizes St. Benedict in two words: *Habitavit secum* ("He dwelt with himself"). No doubt many have lived in monasteries who did not possess this secret. "I approve the life of those men," Ivo of Chartres says of the solitaries, "but neither the deepest forest nor

[54] Cf. Phil. 4:7.

the highest mountain can give happiness to a man if he has not in himself the solitude of the soul, peace of conscience and elevation of heart."

Aristotle defined a man as a social being, and he added, "He who lives alone is either a god or a beast." Christian philosophy has endorsed this verdict while varying its terms: "Who lives alone is either an angel or a devil." According to the Ancren Rule, it was possible for the disturbances of the world to find their way even among the anchoresses. "People say of anchoresses that almost every one of them hath an old woman to feed her ears — a magpie that chatters to her of everything she sees or hears; so it is a common saying: 'From miln and from market / From smithy and from nunnery / Men bring tidings.' This is a sad tale, that a nunnery should be evened to those three places in which there is most idle discourse."

St. Francis de Sales was fond of insisting that places, situations, and conditions had not, in themselves, a great deal to do with our sanctification. He refused to take the side of country life against town life, and warned us against thinking that it is impossible to preserve peace amid bustle and turmoil. "Let us belong to God even in the thick of the disturbance stirred up round about us by the diversity of human affairs. True virtue is not always nourished in external calm any more than good fish are always found in stagnant waters."

"There is a time to speak and a time to be silent." "Silence is the eternal duty of a man," said Carlyle. This is a characteristic exaggeration; nevertheless silence may sometimes be a very peremptory duty. St. John the Silent is so called because for years he concealed the fact that he was a bishop. Humility imposed this secret upon him; and charity and justice impose their secrets upon us. St. Bernadette, at the time of the apparitions, was hardly more than a child. Yet, she faithfully kept the secrets confided to her by God's Mother and carried them with her to the grave. St. John Nepomucen was martyred for refusing to break the secret of the confessional. In art, he is sometimes represented with a padlock on his lips. We all have secrets that we are bound to keep; and there are occasions in our lives when we would do well to place our itching tongues under the protection of St. Bernadette and St. John Nepomucen.

"A good work talked about before the time is half-destroyed" is St. Vincent de Paul's caution to those overly fond of publicity.

"Do not be always saying, 'I did this; I said that'": this is St. Philip Neri's caution to those who are too fond of the personal pronoun.

Chapter Thirteen

⁀

The Saints and Cleanliness

The saints were certainly not fastidious, and to speak of their cleanliness would be disrespectful and would imply a sneaking sort of regard for the foolish charge sometimes brought against them. Indeed, St. Margaret Mary uses the word herself: "I was so excessively dainty that the least want of cleanliness caused me acute nausea." It is true that some of the saints mortified their sensitiveness severely. Bl. Angela of Foligno, for example, did some extraordinary things when, after her conversion, she tended the sick in the hospital of Florence. But she did these things precisely because she was by nature an unusually delicate and dainty woman — so much so that, in her worldly days, her delicacy and daintiness had been the occasion of many of her sins.

If the saints courageously faced the disgusting and the revolting, they did so not because they liked the disgusting and the revolting, but because they did not. When St. Thérèse of the Infant Jesus was splashed by the dirty water from the tub of the Sister who was working next to her in the laundry, she did not like it at all. On the contrary, "my impulse was to draw back and wipe my face in order to show how I disliked it."

St. Vincent de Paul, when he began his task of doing something for the thirty thousand destitute people in the Paris of his day, would enter hovels infested with disease and dirt; but one of the first things he set about doing was to sweep and scour them. He loved always to have about him what he called "spotlessness." Indeed, if such a man can be said to have been "faddy," this was his fad.

Even the most startling austerities of the saints had some very good motives behind them; but we may be quite certain that the motive was never mere indifference to the dirty and the noisome. We are told of St. Juliana of Falconieri, of Bl. Angela, and of others that they frequently dealt with the sores and ulcers of the patients in the hospitals as poor mothers even in our day sometimes deal with the sores and ulcers of their children. But such acts were much more than acts of mortification. They were acts of very heroic charity — acts quite as heroic and practical as the giving of a pint of one's blood to save another's life. Lancing and fomentations were not well understood in the days of those saints, and the courage of such women may have saved many a life.

It is related that the kiss of St. Martin healed the sores of sick people. This particular mortification of St. Martin was, therefore, a very practical mortification. Again, we are told that St. Macarius the Solitary exposed himself for six months to the stings of the most disgusting insects. Our generation need not be expected to appreciate such an example; but our generation might possibly be interested to know that St. Macarius did this as a penance for the impatience and cruelty he had shown to some of those very tormentors.

True, some of the saints were less particular than others; some were not particular at all; and none were quite as particular as are we. It is only recently that the world has grown really particular about such matters. Dr. Johnson was perfectly indifferent to them; and long after his time, tubbing and dressing were still associated only with fops and dandies and the idle rich. Even our grandfathers would have been profoundly shocked to see the young men of our day seriously occupied with face massage and manicures and hair waves and skin lotions. Rightly or wrongly, this sort of thing was considered effeminate by our forefathers. For example, one of St. Ignatius's novice masters reported very unfavorably of a novice who was forever washing his hands. St. Ignatius, it is true, took the part of the novice, but in doing so he was far ahead of his age.

"Damien was a dirty man": this is what his reverend critics said of him. But the critic was a Scot, and Scotch people have their own ideas about dirt. Fr. Damien, however, was a Belgian, and he was an ordinary Belgian brought up in the Belgian way. And, besides, Fr. Damien was living on a small, isolated island with eight hundred lepers to look after. He was not only their chaplain; he was their doctor and their nurse, and often he had to be their undertaker. His critic, on the other hand, was living in a very smart parsonage, which no doubt had "all the latest conveniences with h. and c. laid on and drains by X.Y.Z. and Company."

St. Teresa of Avila detested dirt and untidiness. There may have been a certain amount of both in the Spain of her day, but she insisted on keeping them out of her convents. She was very fond of white linen. Not only did she love holy water, as did St. Margaret Mary ("How I love holy water"); but ordinary water she loved above all the elements. In her *Interior Castle*, when she has to treat of spiritual matters difficult to explain, she falls back upon the metaphor of water. "I can find no simile more appropriate than water to explain spiritual things," and she adds, "I love this element so much that I have studied it more attentively than the others." This attraction was developed in her as a child. She tells us that her nursery contained a picture of the Samaritan woman at the well,[55] that she never tired of looking at it and would often say to our Lord, "Lord, give me of that water."

Of St. Francis of Assisi the *Mirror of Perfection* says, "Next to fire he did specially love water." Heedless though he was of his own comfort, he liked to see cleanliness and seemliness about him. When he was going through the towns and villages of Umbria preaching the gospel of poverty and love, he used to carry a broom with him to sweep the churches that were not so clean as they might have been. "For Francis was grieved whensoever he saw any church that was not so clean as he would have it."

At St. Damian's, the little cell in which he lay sick of an infirmity of the eyes was infested by mice. They ran about him by day and night and would allow him neither to pray nor to eat. Of course, he would not molest them because he never molested any of God's creatures; but he suffered intensely. "Seeing himself thus tormented and moved with pity for his own case, he said within himself, 'Lord, look upon me and succor me in mine infirmities.'"

He accepted and wore the elegant pair of slippers that St. Clare had made to protect his wounded feet from the dirt. He always made a very strong point of good manners — "All are agreed that politeness flowed from him from the first, like one of the public fountains in such a sunny Italian marketplace" — and good manners are the marks of refinement and delicacy. When he was dying, he was very anxious that his body should be laid out in a fresh, clean shroud, and so he dispatched a messenger to his devoted friend the Lady Jacqueline asking her to send at once a roll of ash-colored cloth out of which the Brethren might make him a new habit.

---

[55] See John 4:6 ff.

The Saints and Cleanliness

We find the same solicitude much later on and much nearer home, in our own St. John Fisher. On the morning of his execution, he took unusual pains with his toilet, put off the hair-shirt he always wore, and called for fresh linen. He bade his servant fetch his best fur-lined tippet. All this he called "getting ready for his marriage." The Lieutenant of the Tower meanwhile marveled that he should take such trouble: "What need is there to be so careful about a body that has only one hour to live?" But the martyr answered, "I will keep myself as well as I can until the very hour of my execution."

The Curé of Ars was charged with being rather dirty. But although St. John Vianney wore shoes and cassock until they fell to pieces, dirty he never was. The laundress who looked after the presbytery linen deposed that "he had a natural love for neatness and cleanliness and very frequently changed his personal linen."

Everything about St. Philip Neri was scrupulously clean and tidy. We are told that for some time he could not bring himself to say Mass with a chalice that had been used by another priest; and that he had a drinking cup of his own.

St. Bernard used to say, "Poverty has always pleased me; but dirt, never."

The famous letter that St. Augustine wrote to the nuns at Hippo in 423 is regarded as the foundation of his religious Rule. In it he says, "Keep your clothes carefully, and shake them out for protection against moths. Let your garments be washed either by yourselves or by the washerwoman. Let the bathing of the body not be incessant but be granted once a month, and oftener in case of illness. Let all do what has to be done for the care of health." Certainly, in the directions of both St. Augustine and St. Jerome, we do come across strong recommendations against the use of baths. But baths in those days commonly meant *public* baths, and the public baths had a very bad name. The public baths, indeed, were often the only baths available, as we gather from St. Augustine, who says, "When they [the nuns] go to the baths, let there be not fewer than three."

In the Rule of St. Benedict we find very prudent common sense: "Let baths be granted to the sick as often as shall be expedient." In winter the cowl is to be of thick cloth and in summer of fine. Those who are sent on a journey shall get clean stockings from the common wardrobe, and on returning home, they are to see that they are well washed before being put back in their place. On Saturdays there has to be a tidying up all round. Everything has to be cleaned; the towels are to be washed and even the feet of the monks.

"Be content with your clothes," the Ancren Rule says, "whether they be white or black," but it adds, "See that they be warm and well made — the skins well tawed, and have as many as you need for bed and also for back. Wash yourselves at your pleasure. Have your hair cut four times a year to disburden your heads." It will certainly not surprise us to hear the good bishop telling these women to be content with their clothes; but who would expect to find the hair-cutting item in a book written in the thirteenth century and written for nuns? Even in the eighth century — in the Dark Ages — we find among the little gifts that St. Boniface was fond of sending with the letters he wrote to his friends the nuns a pair of towels. They would send verses, and he would send towels.

"Let us," as St. Benedict says, "have moderation in all things" — even in tidiness and cleanliness. "Be not too finical; but yet be clean," as Dryden says. Tubbing and scrubbing can be carried too far. There is such a thing as good honest dirt, as there is such a thing as good honest sweat. The class of society that has nothing else to do from morning to night but keep itself spruce and spotless has never been of very much use to mankind. The saying "Cleanliness is next to godliness," has really nothing to recommend it except its emphasis. There was nothing godly about the Pharisees, indefatigable washers though they were. "You make clean the outside of the platter; but your inside is full of rapine and corruption." "The things which come forth from the heart, those things defile a man. But to eat with unwashed hands doth not defile a man."[56] Is it not notorious that vice exerts itself in order to look trim and nice and respectable, thinking no doubt to lose "half its guilt by losing all its grossness"?[57]

[56]Cf. Luke 11:39; Matt. 15: 18, 20.
[57]Cf. Edmund Burke, *Reflections on the Revolution in France*.

Chapter Fourteen

~

The Littleness of the Saints

Familiarity with secular history led the late Lord Acton to say, "Most great men have been bad men." In the splendid careers of the makers of history, virtue has a very lean time, as a rule; and what disappoints us in the lives of prominent and much-applauded personages is their neglect of what is called "small behavior." Wholly intent upon the startling and the grandiose, they apparently left to their menials the menial virtues of candor and sincerity and truthfulness and so on. Those who can afford to keep a valet are seldom heroes in the eyes of the valet; and perhaps that is the reason.

Rousseau has been charged with claiming, as the reward of his genius and fine writing, an exemption from nearly all the natural virtues. "He borrowed and begged and never repaid. He betrayed his friends, insulted his benefactors, put his children in the workhouse, and was guilty of every species of meanness." Frederick said of Voltaire's visit to Germany, "He behaved here like a consummate cheat and scoundrel." It is very clear from the life of Napoleon that he had no use whatever for the dictum of Holy Writ: "He that ruleth his own spirit is better than he that taketh cities."

Now, what made the saints saints was neither their exploits nor their miracles, but their virtues; and their virtues were the ordinary commonplace virtues of everyday life. St. John of the Cross is sometimes called the "Doctor of Nothingness," owing to the stress he laid not only upon humility but upon the plain and homespun virtues associated with humble people.

The career and the character of St. Augustine were certainly magnificent, yet it is to him that we owe the advice: "Do you wish to be great? Then begin by being humble. Do you desire to construct a lofty fabric? Then think first about the foundation of humility."

"Be great in little things" was the motto of St. Francis Xavier — a motto he had learned from St. Ignatius.

"Attention to little things is a great thing," said St. John Chrysostom.

"Nothing is small," said St. Teresa, "if God accepts it." And again, "Nothing is small for a great love." So her devotion to holy water is well known, and she declared that there was enough life in a single rubric to throw the soul into an ecstasy.

Again, St. Francis of Assisi is famous among other things for his politeness. St. Francis de Sales was always on his guard against what he called the showy virtues and attracted to those whose practice was frequent, common, and ordinary.

It was objected to St. John Berchmans that he had worked no miracles and had only kept his rule. "Bring me," said the Pope, "a hundred students who have kept their rule, and I shall canonize them all."

Certainly, the saints did not become saints by working miracles; if they worked miracles it was because, in other ways, they had first become saints. And in their zeal for penance and austerity, they did not neglect the lesser although far more important things. "Penance is good," one of them said, "but humility is far better." St. Simeon the Stylite was prepared to leave his pillar at a sign from authority. "Come down," his superior said, and at once his foot was on the rung of the ladder.

The whole lesson of St. Thérèse's "Little Way" is just this. She confessed that she had not the strength to emulate the great ascetics; that she found it very difficult even to keep awake during meditation; but she consoled herself by leaning with all her weight upon the smaller opportunities that presented themselves.

Indeed, the big occasion and the dramatic situation are never really good tests of any virtue. To rescue a drowning person is an act of charity, but being something in the nature of a heroic act, it might be accompanied by a glow of romantic satisfaction that makes it more of a pleasure than anything else. But there is nothing romantic about keeping one's temper; and no one, except God, can possibly applaud us when we repress an uncharitable thought. But there it is: we glow with enthusiasm in reading of the heroic actions of God's servants; then around the corner comes some paltry occasion of practicing the very same virtue in a small way, and we begin to think that virtue is a drab and colorless affair after all.

The humblest lot affords room for the noblest living; and the calendar of the saints proves it. There is St. Baldomer the locksmith, St. Godrich the peddler, St. Andronicus the barber, St. Margaret of Louvain the barmaid, St. Alexander the charcoal-burner, and Bl. Sebastian Doly the carman. Bl. Nuncio Sulprica was a blacksmith's apprentice. St. Aquila and St. Priscilla were tent makers. St. Margaret of Cortona, like Bl. Anna Maria Taigi, was a dressmaker. St. Severus was a weaver, and St. Benedict Joseph was a beggar. SS. Processus, Martinian, Apollinaris, Acestes, Basilides and Varus were jailers. St. Wilfrid was a baker, St. Blaise a wool-comber, and St. Hervaeus was a blind street singer whose companion, strangely enough, was not a dog but a wolf.

Such examples have never been wanting in the Church. They were notorious in St. Augustine's time. "See," he says in his *Confessions*, "how the unlearned start up and take Heaven by storm while we with all our learning grovel upon the earth." And centuries later, St. Anselm declared, "God often works more by the illiterate seeking the things that are God's than by the learned seeking the things that are their own."

Truly, in order to be holy it is not necessary to be great. To be good and just and God-fearing, it is not necessary to leave the world or to change our condition. It is not even necessary to be grown up. St. Imelda was only thirteen; St. Amilina was only twelve; St. Rumwald was only an infant in arms; and he was, besides, an English prince, so we have the glory of having produced the only canonized baby saint — the Holy Innocents, of course, excepted.

Sanctity is by no means a mere question of favorable surroundings. We have already seen how St. Francis de Sales spoke up in favor of city-life and how strongly he insisted upon the possibility of sanctifying any state of life. St. Ives and St. Aprus were lawyers; St. Julian was an innkeeper; St. John of God was a bookseller; St. Odran was chauffeur or, at any rate, chariot-driver to St. Patrick; and, of course, many doctors have been canonized.

St. Omobono was a shopkeeper of whom fortunately we know a good deal. "Trade," says Alban Butler, "is often looked upon as an occasion of lying, frauds, and injustice. That these are the vices of men and not the faults of their profession is clear from the example of this saint." He is the patron of Cremona, and his feast is kept on November 13. Omobono, it seems, was a very successful businessman who made money while telling the truth to his customers and bridling the tradesman's lust for excessive profits. He was also, we are told, exact and assiduous in keeping his accounts, so that his sanctity evidently did not interfere with his business sense.

SS. Gelasius, Genesius, Porphyrius, and Andalion were actors converted, some of them, when actually on the stage and later dying as martyrs.

The saints of the kitchen are in a class by themselves, and a large class it is. Art represents St. Martha holding a soup ladle; and no doubt she can best guide the hands of all those who stir saucepans and upon whom the very lives of so many depend. But she has had a great following. There is a St. Peter who was a cook — and a treasure of a cook, because he was content with a very small salary. SS. Ariadna, Matrona, Radegund, and Agatha were kitchen maids.

St. Agathoclia was a lady's maid. St. Alexis, unknown to his parents, was employed for thirty years as a handyman, doing odd jobs in return for his board and his lodging in a recess under the stairs. St. Zita is the patron of all Christian servants. In the beginning she was a drudge, but by her patience and her efficiency, she won the esteem of her employer and was promoted to the management of the entire household. St. Thecla is said to have been housekeeper to St. Paul, and St. Petronilla housekeeper to St. Peter; so the heroic and long-suffering souls who keep house for busy and poverty-stricken priests have at least two special advocates in Heaven.

Although few details of these saints have come down to us, we may be quite sure that they did not spend their time talking about "the tyranny of the kitchen"; and since they were perfect servants, all those who employ servants will no doubt approve of their canonization. At any rate, their souls were sanctified by means of very

humdrum and commonplace observances. "God," said St. Teresa,
"walks among the pots and pipkins."

Perhaps it does not surprise us to know that there were many
sainted shepherds and shepherdesses, such as SS. Aemilian, Druon,
Germaine Cousin, Solange, and Genevieve. An old proverb maintains that God is accustomed to take His prophets from the
sheepfold. The prophet Amos, for example, was so taken; and St.
Patrick, St. Cuthbert, St. Joan of Arc, and St. Bernadette kept
sheep at one time or another.

But it is very striking to find slaves in the calendar of the saints
and to find so many of them. At a time when, by law, slaves had no
rights and in consequence were subjected to the most barbarous
treatment, the Church was raising them to her altars and publicly
honoring them as martyrs.

SS. Luppus, Guiperius, Mitrius, Blandina, Laurentia, Revocatus, Saturninus, and Secundulus were slaves. St. Onesimus, the
much-loved friend of St. Paul, was a slave. Some, such as SS.
Protus, Hyacinth, and Seraphia, converted their pagan masters
and mistresses and together with them suffered martyrdom. When
St. Melania set up her community of nuns, many of her own slaves
joined it and rose to great heights of sanctity. The effect of all this
upon public opinion must have been tremendous. Henceforth we
hear no more of masters fattening their lampreys with the blood of
slaves, as Pollio, the friend of Augustus, did; or of mistresses carrying at their girdles daggers with which they punished the clumsi-
ness of their domestics. Slowly but surely, thanks entirely to the
action of the Church, these poor creatures recovered their rights
until, under Constantine, stringent laws were passed for their
protection.

Our state of life might not afford any scope for dramatic or romantic actions, but it does afford abundant scope for the exercise

of the virtues that produce saints. There is this to be said for a humble position: if it deprives us of the opportunity of doing more good, it also preserves us from the temptation of doing more harm.

Chapter Fifteen

⁓

The Saints and Sleep

We must be sure that even the most mortified among the saints were as glad to get to bed as we are. "When a man really loves God," St. Philip Neri said, "he comes to such a state in the end that he is obliged to say, 'Lord, let me get some sleep.' "

One of the Psalms has this verse: "The saints shall be joyful on their beds";[58] and if this refers to Paradise, then, in one of the others, David says, "I have remembered Thee upon my bed."[59]

St. Thérèse, in her *Histoire d'une âme*, confides all her weaknesses to us and among them that she used to doze during the morning meditation. "But I reflect that little children awake or asleep are equally dear to their parents." The Gospel can find some excuse even for the three Apostles who slept in the Garden of Gethsemane, leaving our Lord to watch alone. "Their eyes were heavy," it says; and our Lord Himself, although He mildly rebuked them, did not wake them up. "Sleep on now, and take your rest."[60]

[58] Cf. Ps. 149:5.
[59] Ps. 62:7 (RSV = Ps. 63:6).
[60] Matt. 26:43, 45.

St. Clement the Pope, a disciple of St. Peter, tells us that the apostle was fond of recalling details of our Lord's goodness to His disciples, and among them, that when He was traveling with them through Judea, He would often visit them during the night to make sure that they were warm and well covered.

The early ascetics certainly made heroic efforts to confine sleep within the narrowest possible limits; but needless to say, they were never able to dispense with this necessity. It is related of St. Christine, St. Colette, St. Catherine of Ricci, St. Elphide, St. Flore, Bl. Agatha of the Cross, and others that they lived for long periods without the blessing of sleep. This, however, was a miraculous privilege akin to that of those who lived without any other nourishment than the Holy Eucharist.

St. Macarius is said to have gone without sleep for twenty days at a time; St. Dorotheus kept himself awake at night by making mats, and St. Jerome tells us how, when sleep crept over him in spite of his efforts, he dashed himself upon the ground. St. Catherine of Siena took a short sleep only every two nights, and this she called "Paying the debt of sleep to the body." St. Martin of Tours usually slept on the ground, and St. Paula never slept in bed, even during illness. For fifteen years, St. Pachomius took his repose sitting upon a stone. St. Charles Borromeo usually slept in a chair or on the top of the bed in his clothes. When at last he was induced to get right into bed, he insisted on having a mattress of straw. He is responsible for one of the chilliest pieces of advice ever given by a saint: "The best way not to find the bed too cold is to go to bed colder than the bed is."

But, of course, such extremes must be judged not by *our* ideas of comfort and convenience, but by theirs. These saints lived in very robust times and in much warmer climates than ours; and, after all, the bed matters but little, provided there is sound and refreshing sleep. Probably they slept far more soundly than do we. And others besides saints have managed very well with a small amount of sleep. Napoleon could go for a week without sleeping as we understand it. He had acquired the knack of being able to drop off to sleep at odd moments, and those odd moments kept him going for days. Cardinal Mezzofanti, the great linguist, never slept for more than three hours. Castel, the author of the *Heptaglot Lexicon*, for twenty years slept but four hours each day. Suarez did with even less; and our own Sir Matthew Hale maintained that six hours was more than enough for all. St. Philip Neri took four hours or at most five. Matt Talbot went to bed at 10:30 and rose at two o'clock.[61] Although St. Francis de Sales was fond of saying, "We shall have all eternity in which to rest," he had five hours' sleep as a rule. The Curé of Ars slept for three hours.

Sleep is like food; some require more than others, and the quantity of each is very largely a matter of custom. We find no difficulty in persuading ourselves that we require a good deal of both; and the saints, with like facility, persuaded themselves that they required very little. Nature is very adaptable. It is astonishing what we can quite conveniently do without when it comes to the point, and it is perhaps safe to say that the system accustoms itself with greater ease to privations than to excesses. Gradual and systematic practice made their mortifications a second nature to the saints. We have already seen with what prudence St. Simeon habituated himself to his perch on the top of the pillar; and it is related of St. Peter of Alcantara that he inured himself to his vigils by degrees, taking care that they should never be prejudicial to his health.

[61] Matt Talbot (1856-1925), alcoholic who converted and devoted the rest of his life to prayer, fasting, and service.

And, besides, the saints had this enormous advantage: their minds and hearts were in a habitual state of tranquility. Nothing exhausts the springs of our vitality more readily than our disorderly passions, our inordinate ambitions, and the multiplicity of our desires. The saints were free from the guilty worries and anxieties that undermine the repose of the worldly. They had that most restful of all pillows: a good conscience. If the truth were known, perhaps St. Peter of Alcantara had in a week more hours of genuine natural sleep than many of the butterflies of society enjoy in a month.

The saints never hesitated to deprive themselves of sleep and rest in the interest of what they conceived to be duty or charity. There is nothing fanatical about that, because men and women of the world do the same for their own ends. The House of Commons thinks nothing of protracting its sittings right through the night. People will sit all night in a queue at the doors of a theater. During the trial of Marie Antoinette, as Belloc relates, "none in the staring audience that watched the slow determination of the business would suffer the approach of sleep."

At the other end of the scale are the Seven Sleepers who slept for two hundred years. According to St. Gregory of Tours, they were citizens of Ephesus who, in the year 250, were walled up in a cavern so that they might be starved to death. A century later, when controversy was raging in the neighborhood, they came out and bore witness to the traditional teaching of the Church against the novelties of the heretics. The tradition of this miracle was so widespread that the Sleepers are mentioned in the Koran; and it is thought to have suggested to Longfellow his tale of Rip Van Winkle. The names of the Sleepers were Maximian, Marcus, Martinianus, Dionysius, John, Serapion, and Constantine. The Greeks and all other Eastern Churches include the Seven Sleepers in their catalogs of saints. Butler is inclined to regard the story as largely legend, but there is no doubt that for hundreds of years it obtained universal credence.

The prudent Rule of St. Benedict allowed each monk a mat, a blanket, a rug, and a pillow. They were also commanded to sleep in their habits, and from the point of view of comfort, this must have been an improvement on the common custom of sleeping without nightclothes of any description. St. Jerome's pillow, like Jacob's, was made of stone; but St. Francis of Assisi had a feather pillow that the Brethren compelled him to use on account of the infirmity of his eyes. When he was in the hermitage at Greccio and could not sleep, he blamed the Devil for it. "I do perceive that this Devil is passing crafty, forasmuch as not being able to do a hurt unto my soul, he is fain to hinder a necessity of my body in such sort that I cannot sleep, and by this means to hinder the cheerfulness of my heart."

Those who find it difficult to get up in the morning — that is to say, nearly everybody — will rejoice to know that there is a saint who makes it his business to come to the rescue of this particular infirmity. He is St. Vitus, or Guy, a martyr who suffered in the fourth century and whose very appropriate symbol is a rooster.

A monastic chronicle tells us of a saintly old woman employed to ring the bell for the offices of the Church of St. Romuald in Malines. The chronicle praises the fidelity and the punctuality of this woman and relates as a thing to be remembered and extolled that she kept a rooster to serve as an alarm clock, lest she might fail in her duty. If she had been canonized, she would certainly be par excellence *the* patron of all sluggards.

Should this book fall into the hands of the bedridden, it will console such to know that there were saints, and many of them, who did little else here below except sanctify their sick beds. Anne

Catherine Emmerich, Bl. Anna Maria Taigi, St. Veronica Guiliani, and St. Marie Frances were bedridden. Bl. Marie Bagnesi, the Dominican tertiary, was for forty-five years prostrated by illness and, according to the Bollandists, had hardly one of her members intact. St. Frica was confined to bed with paralysis for six years; and we are told that she suffered intensely from the rats that attacked her when her mother was out in the town begging for bread.

Of all these sufferers, St. Lydwine of Schiedam is the most famous. Born in Holland at the end of the fourteenth century, she fell while skating at the age of fifteen and contracted a disease that confined her to her bed for the remainder of her life: thirty-five years. Yet nothing was able to shake the fortitude of this heroic soul. Afflicted though she was by maladies that utterly baffled and bewildered the medical science of her day, she entreated our Lord not to spare her, and she obtained from Him the grace of expiating the sins of others by means of her own sufferings. And He indeed heard her prayer. She was endowed with wonderful supernatural powers. Angels attended on her. Our Lord Himself gave her Holy Communion. At the hour of her death, He stood by her side, and restored her body to its former condition of soundness; her vanished beauty reappeared; sick people came in crowds to her bedside: and great miracles were wrought. It was examples of this kind that moved Fr. Faber to ask, "Will anyone say that a valetudinarian cannot be a saint or practice heroic virtue?"

It is very doubtful if sickness will ever be banished from the world. In spite of the admirable efforts of science, there is still disease and deformity. Very few are quite as well as they would like to be, and some are more unfortunate than others. St. Teresa thought that there ought to be an invalid in every community; and perhaps God will always permit chronic infirmity to fall upon this one or that in order to give His creatures an opportunity of glorifying

Him by their patience and resignation. "Sickness," said one of the saints, "sanctifies quicker than anything else" — yes, if it is rightly understood and accepted in a supernatural spirit. Sometimes it is God's last resource in His providential plan of saving us, and if it fails, our case is very desperate indeed.

Bad health is not a blessing, by any means. But if ill health comes, in spite of all our care, we can, at least, make a virtue of its necessity, as God's servants did, one of whom said, "To carry the Cross is to make the Cross carry us."

Chapter Sixteen

⌒

The Secret of the Saints

On winter evenings, have you never spent some bittersweet moments by the fireside, in tracing the features of the absent in the glow of the embers? A mysterious artist seems to be at work among the red-hot coals, and by a process of his own, he uses the spirals of smoke and the jets of gas to draw visionary images on the canvas of the flaming fuel. Your own imagination does the rest; and out of the flickering lights and shadows, you build up the faces of distant or buried friends — "those blessed household countenances cleansed from the dishonor of the grave." Leaning back in the chair, you seem to see kind glances shining out of the retrospect, and to hear the tones of voices long silent.

And who would say that such fanciful musings are always unprofitable? Perhaps the soul gains fresh vigor from the recollections with which they are associated. They transport us into the midst of the innocence and enthusiasm of our childhood and youth. We are permitted, for a moment, to breathe again the wholesome breath of the springtime and early morning of life. We are not only consoled; we are purified. The harsh in us is toned down a little, and the sour is sweetened; and before that past, of which a glimpse has been vouchsafed to us, we bow our heads with respect and with veneration.

Now, in holy Scripture, fire is the element most frequently associated with God and with the things of God; and, above all, it is identified with His attribute of sanctity. God appears to Moses in a burning bush. On Sinai, to Ezekiel, to Isaiah, and to St. John, He reveals Himself in the midst of flames. He cleanses the lips of His prophet with a red-hot coal. His chariot is composed of fire, according to the psalmist; and His Word and His Church are compared to fire by Jeremiah. And fire is pre-eminently the symbol of His holiness. It was the fire of sanctity that our Lord came, as He said, to kindle upon the earth. John the Baptist described His baptism as a baptism of fire; and the Holy Spirit, the Sanctifier, the Inspiration of all holy lives and holy actions, the Molder and Fashioner of the saints, came down, in the first instance, in the form of parted tongues "as it were of fire."[62]

In a very real sense, therefore, the faces of all the saints look out at us from the midst of the fire of God's love and perfection. They are the coals that the psalmist says are lighted by the fire that flames from the throne of the Most High. They are the "sparks that fly upward"; the "torches of lighted fire" described in the book of Job.[63] "God," says holy Scripture, "is a consuming fire";[64] and a saint's heart is the nearest thing to the sight of God that we know. The saints suffered as a rule — indeed we instinctively look for suffering in their lives — because "the acceptable man must be tried in the furnace of tribulation." Some of them, such as St. Teresa of Avila and St. Gertrude, are represented with a flaming heart. In

[62] Acts 2:3.
[63] Job 41:10.
[64] Cf. Deut. 4:24.

sacred art, St. Brice, the Archbishop of Tours and the disciple of St. Martin, is shown with fire in his hand; St. Anthony the Hermit stands upon fire; his namesake of Padua has a flame issuing from his breast. A modern biographer of the saints called those of them who made themselves victims of expiation, the "Lightning Conductors of Society": "They draw upon themselves the demoniacal fluid; they absorb temptations to vice; they appease the wrath of the Most High so that He may not place the earth under an interdict."[65] Long before him, St. John Chrysostom likened the Fathers of the Desert to lighthouses that serve to guide and cheer us in the midst of the dangers and darkness of life. A letter written by one of her own nuns thus describes St. Madeleine Sophie in her eighty-fifth year: "There is nothing left of her now but a flame of fire." And, best of all, there is the eleventh-century bishop, St. Peter Ignaeus: St. Peter the Fiery.

The respect and love St. Francis had for fire are well known. He carried this reverence so far that he would not quench it even at the risk of a conflagration. When the doctor came to relieve the infirmity in his eye with a cautery, the saint preached it a little sermon bidding it not hurt him too much. "Above all creatures," says the *Mirror of Perfection*, "he did love the Sun and Fire." And again, "Among all insensible creatures he had a special affection for fire, by reason of its beauty and usefulness." "Fire," the saint himself said. "Fire, noble and useful among all nations, I have loved thee and yet will love thee. In the morning, we ought to praise God for Brother Sun, and in the evening, for Brother Fire." "Fire, comely, joyful, masterful, and strong" is his description of it in the "Canticle of the Creatures." The fact is that St. Francis saw in this element the rich type of the love of God that Isaiah describes as "a

---

[65] Joris Karl Huysmans, *En Route*, ch. 1.

devouring flame."[66] It was a constant reminder to him that God desired nothing from us except to be loved in return; as our Lord expressed it: "I am come to cast fire upon the earth, and what will I but that it be kindled."[67]

This indeed is the whole secret of the saints, the explanation of their heroism, the key to the inimitable and puzzling incidents we meet with in their lives. When a heart opens, really opens, to our Lord, He sets it on fire — on fire with the love of Himself. The disciples who walked and talked with Him on the road to Emmaus said the one to the other, "Was not our heart burning within us whilst He spoke in the way?"[68] And He himself described His precursor John the Baptist as "a burning and shining light."[69] When St. Gertrude had her first vision of our Lord in the corridor of her convent, when her glance met His, she felt her heart going hot within her.

A non-Catholic essayist of our own day has written, "Let no one deny to the Church of Rome one mark of the true Church: the power of being able to breed saints." And the source of this never-failing fertility is the Church's dogma of the infinite love of God for man — the astonishing doctrine "that God loves man to the point of passion," as Msgr. Bougaud expresses it.

From time to time, this revealed truth is realized vividly, and then we have a saint; we have a man or a woman devoured and therefore transformed by the fire of Divine Charity. "I see God" were the last words of St. Anthony of Padua, and his dying face became bright and transparent, lighted up by the illumination of his soul.

[66]Cf. Isa. 10:17; 29:6; 30:30.
[67]Luke 12:49.
[68]Luke 24:32.
[69]John 5:35.

The Secret of the Saints

And all the great servants of God had, in one way or another, caught a glimpse of the Divine Beauty. Hence we find them flinging the world aside, trampling upon its joys, its riches, its honors; betaking themselves to solitary places and climbing to the tops of pillars. They have seen the Eternal, and in consequence this world shrinks and appears paltry by comparison, just as it does to the astronomer who is familiar with the dimensions of the other planets and stars. "How base earth grows when I look up to heaven," said St. Ignatius. "Eternity, eternity, eternity" St. Teresa used to repeat to herself as a child. This alone accounts for all their so-called extremes and exaggerations.

True love never calculates. "Love's reasons are without reason." "It is impossible to love and to be wise." "A generous friendship no cold medium knows." As Cardinal Newman said, "I would not give much for that love which is never extravagant." Under the influence of a real affection the human being shoots up into the giant, and sustained as it is by its union with another spirit, it is deterred by no hardship and shrinks from no sacrifice. And there never was a story of a saint that was not in a real sense a love story. "Love is repaid by love alone" was the motto that St. Teresa learned from St. John of the Cross. And in part payment of the infinite love of God, they spent themselves and were spent. The memory of the debt contracted by the human race on Mount Calvary animated and inflamed their hearts.

In short, the lives of the saints are a world of their own, and it is a fiery, flaming world of light and of heat — the sort of world St. Paul lived in who said, "Who is scandalized and I am not on fire?"[70] And each of them, even the humblest and most obscure, in passing from the earth left behind a light peculiar to himself or herself.

[70] 2 Cor. 11:29.

By way of introduction to one of the stories Fr. Faber wrote for children, he said, "How would it do to take angels instead of fairies?" And so it might be a good plan when we sit by the fire to try to see in it the forms and faces of the saints. Perhaps a spark or two of their ardor may come to light up and to warm our own dark and chilly lives. G. K. Chesterton acknowledges that even in his boyhood days, his fancy "caught fire" with the glory of St. Francis of Assisi; indeed St. Bonaventure says of St. Francis, "By the remembrance of the saints, as by the touch of glowing coals of fire, he was kindled and converted into a divine flame."

❧

"As often as you read anything in this book,
greet the Lady with a Hail Mary
for him who wrote it. Moderate enough
I am, who ask so little."

The Ancren Rule

Saints Mentioned or Quoted

We have added this appendix to assist readers who may not be familiar with the saints Fr. Roche mentioned when he wrote this book — years ago. Is some cases, however, we ourselves were unsure of which saint Fr. Roche was considering or were not able to find information beyond the saint's name. In those cases, we have indicated our uncertainty or have simply chosen not to include information that might be inaccurate.

St. Acestes (d. c. 65), soldier who escorted St. Paul to his execution and, converted by him, was later martyred (July 2).

St. Agatha (d. c. 251), virgin martyred in Sicily during the persecution by emperor Decius (February 5).

Bl. Agatha of the Cross (1547-1621), Spanish Dominican.

St. Agathoclia: Christian slave and martyr (September 17).

St. Agnes (d. c. 304), Roman martyr (January 21).

St. Agnes of Assisi (1197-1253), younger sister and follower of St. Clare of Assisi (November 16).

Bl. Agnes of Bohemia (1205-1282), princess who built a hospital, a Franciscan friary, and a convent for Poor Clares, which she later entered and of which she became abbess (March 6).

St. Albert the Great (c. 1200-1280), medieval theologian, philosopher, and scientist (November 15).

St. Aldegunde (c. 630-684), Benedictine abbess and visionary (January 30).

St. Alexander "the charcoal-burner" (c. 275), convert to Christianity who became Bishop of Cormana and was martyred (August 11).

St. Alexis (d. c. early fifth century), son of a wealthy Roman senator, who disguised himself as a beggar and spent his days praying, ministering to others, and teaching catechism to children; known as "The Man of God" (July 17).

St. Alonzo (1532-1617), Spanish wool merchant and Jesuit lay brother; also known as St. Alphonsus Rodriguez (October 30).

St. Aloysius Gonzaga (1568-1591), young Jesuit who cared for plague victims (June 21).

St. Alphonsus Liguori (1696-1787), bishop, Doctor, writer, and founder of the Redemptorists (August 1).

St. Ambrose (c. 340-397), Bishop of Milan and Doctor (December 7).

Bl. Angela of Foligno (c. 1248-1309), widow and mystic (February 28).

Bl. Anne Catherine Emmerich (1774-1824), visionary and stigmatist (February 9).

Bl. Anna Maria Taigi (1769-1837), laywoman, wife, mother, and mystic (June 9).

Ven. Anne de Guigné (1911-1922), difficult, strong-willed child who, at the age of four, experienced profound conversion and dedicated herself to perfect obedience and virtue.

St. Apollinaris (d. c. 290) spectator at the martyrdom of St. Timothy who, moved by Timothy's courage, converted and was martyred (August 23).

St. Anselm (c. 1033-1109), Archbishop of Canterbury and Doctor (April 21).

St. Anthony the Hermit (251-356), desert monk and father of Western monasticism (January 17).

St. Anthony of Padua (1195-1231), Franciscan friar and Doctor (June 13).

St. Apollonia (d. 249), virgin and martyr (February 9).

St. Aprus (d. 507), lawyer who became a priest and Bishop of Toul (September 15).

St. Aquila (first century), Jewish tent-maker and husband of St. Priscilla who converted to Christianity and was martyred. (July 8).

St. Ariadna (d. c. 130), Christian slave considered a martyr (September 17).

St. Athanasius (c. 297-373), Bishop of Alexandria and Doctor (May 2).

St. Augustine (354-430), Bishop of Hippo and Doctor (August 28).

St. Baldomer: a man devoted to God at whose tomb miracles have occurred (February 27).

St. Basil the Great (c. 329-379), Bishop of Cappadocia and Doctor (January 2).

St. Basilides (d. c. 205), Pagan Roman soldier who defended St. Potomiana against a mob as she was led to martyrdom. Having received visions of the saint, he converted and was martyred (June 30).

St. Bavon (589-654), Belgian nobleman who converted from an immoral life after hearing a sermon by St. Amand. He later built an abbey on his estate, gave it to St. Amand, and became a monk there (October 1).

St. Benedict (c. 480- c. 547), abbot who founded the monastery of Monte Cassino (July 11).

St. Benedict Joseph Labre (1748-1783), pilgrim and mendicant saint (April 16).

St. Bernadette (1844-1879), Sister of Notre Dame who, in 1858, received eighteen apparitions of the Blessed Virgin Mary at Lourdes in France (April 16).

St. Bernard of Clairvaux (1090-1153), abbot and Doctor (August 20).

St. Blaise (d. c. 316), bishop of Sebaste and martyr (February 3).

St. Blandina (d. 177), slave and martyr (June 2).

St. Bonaventure (1221-1274), Franciscan mystical theologian and scholastic, writer, bishop, and Doctor (July 15).

St. Boniface (c. 680-754), bishop, Primate of Germany, and martyr (June 5).

St. Brice (d. 444), orphan rescued by St. Martin of Tours and raised by his clerics. He lived a wild and wicked life, became an ambitious priest who had contempt for St. Martin, but eventually changed and began to live a better life (November 13).

St. Camillus of Lellis (1550-1614), reformed soldier and gambler who directed a hospital and founded the nursing congregation of the Ministers of the Sick (July 14).

St. Catherine of Alexandria (d. c. 305), convert who, in turn, converted others to Christianity and was martyred (November 25).

St. Catherine of Ricci (1522-1590), Dominican sister and visionary (February 13).

St. Catherine of Siena (1347-1380), Dominican tertiary (April 29).

St. Cecilia: early Christian martyr and patroness of Church musicians (November 22).

St. Charles Borromeo (1538-1584), bishop who established the Confraternity of Christian Doctrine (November 4).

St. Clare of Assisi (c. 1193-1253), foundress of the Poor Clares (August 11).

St. Clement I (d. 101), fourth Pope, martyr (November 23).

St. Clement Hofbauer (1751-1820), Redemptorist who opened an orphanage and schools and established a Redemptorist congregation in Warsaw (March 15).

St. Colette (1381-1447), foundress of the Colettines, a branch of the Poor Clares (March 6).

St. Columba (c. 521-597), Irish abbot and missionary (June 9).

St. Cosmas (d. c. 283), physician and martyr; brother of St. Damian (September 26).

Curé of Ars (1786-1859), St. John Vianney: patron saint of parish priests (August 4).

St. Cuthbert (c. 634-687), bishop (March 20).

St. Damian (d. c. 283), physician and martyr; brother of St. Cosmas (September 26).

Bl. Damien de Veuster (1840-1889), priest who ministered among the lepers of Molokai (May 10).

St. Dominic (c. 1170-1221), founder of the Dominican Order, also known as the Order of Preachers (August 8).

Bl. Dominic Barberi (1792-1849), Passionist priest who received John Henry Newman into the Church (August 27).

St. Dorotheus (eleventh century), monk (January 5).

St. Dositheus (d. c. 530), pagan convert to Christianity who became a monk and cared for the sick (February 23).

St. Druon (1105-1186), Flemish nobleman who became a penitential pilgrim, was a shepherd for several years, and later became a hermit; also known as St. Drogo (April 16).

St. Dymphna (d. c. 620), a young woman martyred by her father for defending her purity (May 15).

St. Eligius (588-660), Bishop of Noyon and Tournai who converted many (December 1).

St. Elizabeth of Hungary (1207-1231), daughter of King Andreas II of Hungary, niece of St. Hedwig, and widow who became a Franciscan tertiary (November 17).

St. Eusignius (d. 362), soldier martyred at Antioch (August 5).

St. Eustace (d. 188), pagan Roman general in Trajan's army who converted to Christianity after seeing a glowing cross between the antlers of a stag; later martyred (September 20).

St. Felix of Cantalice (1515-1587), Capuchin lay brother (May 18).

St. Francis of Assisi (1182-1226), founder of the Franciscan Order, also known as the Order of Friars Minor (October 4).

St. Francis Borgia (1510-1572), Duke of Gandia who became a Jesuit, established the order throughout western Europe, and sent missionaries to the Americas (October 10).

St. Francis of Paula (1416-1507), founder of the Order of Minim friars (April 2).

St. Francis de Sales (1567-1622), Bishop of Geneva, writer, and Doctor (January 24).

St. Francis Xavier (1506-1552), Jesuit missionary to the East Indies (December 3).

Bl. Frederick Ozanam (1813-1853), founder of the St. Vincent de Paul Society (September 7).

St. Galla (d. c. 550), widow who founded a convent and a hospital and cared for the sick and the poor (October 5).

St. Gelasius (d. c. 304), pagan actor who converted to Christianity and was martyred (August 25).

St. Genesius (d. c. 304), pagan actor who converted to Christianity and was martyred (August 25).

St. Genevieve (c. 420-c. 500), virgin, patroness of Paris (January 3).

St. George (third or fourth century), martyr (April 23).

St. Germaine Cousin (c. 1579-1601), shepherdess (June 15).

St. Gertrude (c. 1256-1302), German mystic (November 16).

St. Gertrude of Nivelles (626-659), abbess, mystic, and visionary (March 17).

St. Giles, Provençal hermit or monk in the sixth or eighth century (September 1).

St. Godric (c. 1065-1170), hermit who began as a peddler (May 21).

St. Gomidas Keumurgian (c. 1656-1707), priest and martyr (November 5).

St. Gregory the Great (d. 604), Pope from 590, writer, and Doctor (September 3).

St. Gregory Nazianzen (c. 329-390), bishop of Constantinople, theologian, and Doctor (January 2).

St. Gregory of Nyssa (d. c. 395), bishop and writer (March 9).

St. Guthlac (c. 673-714), English hermit (April 11).

St. Hervaeus (d. c. 575), Abbot of Plouvien, singer, minstrel, teacher, and miracle-worker (June 17).

Bl. Hildegarde von Bingen (1098-1179), visionary, author, and composer with knowledge of natural history and the medicinal uses of plants, animals, and so forth (September 17).

St. Hippolytus (d. c. 235), Roman priest and theological writer who became an antipope, but was later reconciled to the Church and martyred (August 13).

Holy Innocents (first century), the children killed by Herod in his effort to destroy the Christ Child (December 28).

St. Hubert of Liege (c. 656-727), worldly, dissolute youth who converted and eventually became Bishop of Maastricht (November 3).

St. Hugh of Lincoln (c. 1135-1200), bishop (November 17).

St. Hyacinth (d. c. 257), servant, brother of St. Protus, and martyr (September 11).

St. Hyacintha of Mariscotti (d. 1640), religious who was unfaithful to her rule, converted, relapsed, and finally converted and attained heroic virtue (January 30).

St. Ignatius of Loyola (1491-1556), founder of the Jesuit Order, also known as the Society of Jesus (July 31).

St. Imelda (1322-1333), visionary who miraculously received her First Communion in 1333 and died immediately afterward in ecstasy (May 13).

St. Ives of Kermartin (d. 1303), French lawyer turned priest (May 19).

St. Ivo of Chartres (1040-1116), Bishop of Chartres (May 23).

St. Jane Frances de Chantal (1572-1641), foundress of the Visitation Order (August 18).

St. Jerome (c. 342-420), Doctor who translated the Bible into Latin (September 30).

St. Joan of Arc (1412-1431), French heroine who led the French army against English invaders and was burned to death for alleged heresy, but later declared innocent (May 30).

St. John (first century), Evangelist and one of the Twelve Apostles (December 27).

St. John Berchmans (1599-1621), Jesuit who followed the "Little Way" (November 26).

St. John Bosco (1815-1888), priest who founded the Salesian Order (January 31).

St. John Chalybita (d. c. 450), monk and hermit (January 15).

St. John Chrysostom (c. 347-407), Archbishop of Constantinople and Doctor; named Chrysostom, or "Golden Mouth" for his eloquent preaching (September 13).

St. John of the Cross (1542-1591), Spanish Carmelite mystic, and reformer of the Carmelite Order (December 14).

St. John Fisher (1469-1535), English bishop martyred under King Henry VIII (June 22).

St. John of God (1495-1550), founder of the order of the Brothers Hospitallers (March 8).

St. John Nepomucen (1330-1383), priest who was killed for refusing to violate the seal of Confession (May 16).

Ven. John Henry Newman (1801-1890), Anglican churchman and scholar who converted to Catholicism.

St. John the Silent (454-558), monk known for his great love of silence and recollection (May 13).

St. John Vianney: see Curé of Ars.

Bl. Joseph de Anchieta (1534-1597), Jesuit missionary (June 9).

St. Joseph Calasanctius (1556-1648), founder of the Piarists (August 25).

Ven. Joseph Passerat (1772-1858), successor to St. Clement Hofbauer as Vicar General of the Redemptorists.

St. Julian: pilgrim who, with his wife, built a hospice to care for the sick and the poor (February 12).

St. Juliana of Falconieri (1270-1341), Servite tertiary (June 19).

St. Julie Billiart (1751-1816), virgin, cofoundress of the Institute of Notre Dame of Namur (April 8).

St. Kentigern (c. 518-603), British bishop and abbot (January 13).

St. Laurentia (d. 302), slave of St. Palatias, whom she converted and with whom she was martyred (October 8).

St. Leonard of Port Maurice (1676-1751), Franciscan friar and missioner (November 26).

St. Leonilla (second century), holy woman who converted her grandsons to Christianity and was later martyred with them (January 29).

Little Flower: see St. Thérèse of Lisieux.

St. Louise de Marillac (1591-1660), cofoundress of the Daughters of Charity, now known as the Sisters of Charity of St. Vincent de Paul (March 15).

St. Luke (first century), Evangelist and author of the Acts of the Apostles (October 18).

St. Luppus: slave and martyr (August 23).

St. Lupus of Troyes (c. 383-c. 478), Bishop of Troyes (July 29).

St. Lydwine (1380-1433), virgin who bore patiently the painful symptoms of an illness that resulted from a skating accident and who later received visions (April 14).

St. Macarius the Solitary (c. 300-390), priest who lived an austere life and ministered to his fellow hermits (January 15).

St. Madeleine Sophie Barat (1779-1865), foundress of the Society of the Sacred Heart for the education of girls (May 25).

St. Marcian: perhaps the fourth-century hermit (d. c. 387; November 2).

St. Margaret Mary Alacoque (1647-1690), Visitation nun who received revelations of and promoted devotion to the Sacred Heart of Jesus (October 16).

St. Margaret of Cortona (d. 1297), mother who repented of an illicit relationship with a young nobleman when he died suddenly, became a Franciscan tertiary, received visions, and was the instrument of marvelous healings (February 22).

St. Margaret of Louvain (1207-1225), teenage maid at an inn who had planned to become a Cistercian nun but was murdered by thieves (September 2).

Bl. Marie Bagnesi (1514-1577), Dominican tertiary and visionary (May 27).

Ven. Marie Celeste Crostorosa (1696-1755), founder of the Redemptoristine Order.

St. Marie Frances: perhaps St. Mary Frances of the Five Wounds of Jesus (1715-1791), Franciscan tertiary and stigmatist who suffered various physical ailments (October 6).

St. Martha (first century), friend of Jesus and sister of Mary and Lazarus (July 29).

St. Martin of Porres (1579-1639), South American lay brother and infirmarian at the Dominican friary of the Rosary in Lima, Peru, and friend to the poor (November 3).

St. Martin of Tours (c. 316-397), Bishop of Tours (November 11).

St. Martinian (first century), jailer and martyr.

St. Mary of Egypt (c. 344-c. 421), penitent who retired to the desert to atone for her sins (April 3).

St. Mary Magdalene (first century), follower of Jesus and the first to whom He appeared after His Resurrection (July 22).

St. Matrona: Christian maid of a Jewish mistress, who persecuted her and had her beaten to death (March 15).

St. Mechtilde (c. 1241-1298), teacher of St. Gertrude (February 26).

St. Melania the Older (c. 342-410), patrician woman who founded a monastery on the Mount of Olives in Jerusalem (June 8).

St. Melania the Younger (d. 439), granddaughter of St. Melania the Older; married woman who joined a community of women in Jerusalem, where her husband had become a monk, devoted herself to caring for the poor and copying books (December 31).

St. Mitrius (d. 314), Greek slave and martyr (November 13).

St. Monica (332-387), mother of St. Augustine (August 27).

St. Nicerate (d. c. 405), wealthy Byzantine noblewoman who cared for the sick and the poor and frequently was able to cure people whose doctors had been unable to cure them (December 27).

St. Nilus (910-1005), abbot (September 26).

St. Norbert (1080-1134), Bishop of Magdeburg and founder of the Premonstratensians, or Norbertines (June 6).

Bl. Nuncio Sulprica (1817-1836), blacksmith's apprentice known for his great virtue (May 5).

St. Odran (d. c. 452), St. Patrick's chariot driver who, according to legend, spotted an ambush, traded places with St. Patrick, and died in the attack meant for St. Patrick (February 19).

St. Omobono (d. 1197), businessman who supported the poor with his work (November 13).

St. Onesimus (d. c. 90), slave of St. Philemon converted by St. Paul (February 16).

St. Pachomius (c. 290-c. 346), first monk to organize hermits around a written rule and shared community life (May 14).

St. Pantaleon (d. c. 305), Christian physician and martyr (July 27).

St. Paschal Baylon (1540-1592), Franciscan friar (May 17).

St. Patrick (c. 389-c. 461), patron saint and apostle of Ireland (March 17).

St. Paul (d. 67), Apostle and author of several New Testament letters (June 29).

St. Paul the Hermit (c. 230-c. 342), desert hermit buried by St. Anthony the Abbot (January 15).

St. Paula (347-404), wife and mother of five — among them SS. Blesilla and Eustochium — who, after her husband's death, formed a community of religious women and helped St. Jerome in his biblical work (January 26).

St. Peregrine Laziosi (1260-1345), Servite priest who was miraculously cured of cancer (May 1).

St. Perpetua (third century), young married woman and martyr (March 7).

St. Peter (first century), one of the Twelve Apostles and the first Pope (June 29; Chair of Peter: February 22).

St. Peter of Alcantara (1499-1562), mystic and founder of a reformed order of Franciscans known as the Alcantarines (October 19).

Peter the Hermit (c. 1050-1115), eloquent French preacher at the time of the Crusades.

St. Petronilla (first century), housekeeper of St. Peter and martyr (May 31).

St. Philip Benizi (1233-1285), Servite priest who worked for peace between the Guelphs and the Ghibellines and assisted at the second general Council of Lyons (August 23).

St. Philip Neri (1515-1595), Italian priest who founded the Congregation of the Oratory (May 26).

St. Philomena (d. c. 304), thirteen-year-old virgin who was martyred for resisting the advances of the Emperor Diocletian (August 11).

St. Pius V (1504-1572), Pope from 1565 (April 30).

St. Pius X (1835-1914), Pope from 1903 (August 21).

St. Polycarp (d. c. 155), bishop and martyr (February 23).

St. Porphyrius (d. 362), actor and martyr (September 15).

St. Prisca: see St. Priscilla.

St. Priscilla (first century), Jewish tent-maker, wife of St. Aquila, and martyr (July 8).

St. Processus (first century), jailer and martyr.

St. Procopius (c. 980-1053), priest, hermit, and abbot (July 4).

St. Protus (d. c. 257), servant, brother of St. Hyacinth, and martyr (September 11).

St. Quirinus (d. c. 117), jailer who converted to Christianity and was martyred (March 30).

St. Radegund (518-587), Queen of Thuringia who founded and lived at the convent of the Holy Cross in Poitiers (August 13).

St. Revocatus (d. 203), slave and martyr (March 6).

St. Robert Bellarmine (1542-1621), Jesuit Cardinal, teacher, writer, and Doctor (September 17).

St. Roch (1295-1327), French pilgrim to Rome who cared for plague victims and was mistakenly accused of and imprisoned for espionage (August 16).

St. Romuald (c. 950-1027), founder of the Camaldolese Order (February 7).

St. Rumwald (c. 650), son of the Christian Saint Cyneburga and the pagan Alchfrid of Northumbria; lived only three days, during which time he repeated several times, "I am a Christian" and asked for Baptism and Holy Communion (August 28 or November 3).

St. Saturninus (d. 203), slave and martyr (March 6).

St. Scholastica (480-543), nun and twin sister of St. Benedict (February 10).

St. Sebastian: early Christian martyr (January 20).

St. Secundulus (d. 203), slave and martyr (March 6).

St. Seraphia (d. 119), Syrian slave and martyr (July 29).

St. Servulus (d. c. 590), layman and paraplegic (December 23).

St. Severus of Ravenna (d. c. 348), poor weaver who became Bishop of Ravenna (February 1).

St. Silvester I (c. 270-335), Pope (December 31).

St. Simeon Stylites (c. 390-459), hermit (January 5).

St. Solange (d. c. 880), young shepherdess martyred for resisting the advances of her landlord (May 10).

St. Stanislaus (1030-1079), bishop of Krakow and martyr (April 11).

St. Teresa of Avila (1515-1582), Spanish Carmelite nun, Doctor, and mystic who reformed her order (October 15).

St. Thecla (first century), follower of St. Paul (September 23).

St. Théophane Vénard (d. 1861), priest of the Missions Étrangères of Paris who was sent to Western Tonking, where he suffered persecution, imprisonment, and martyrdom (February 2).

St. Thérèse of Lisieux (1873-1897), Carmelite nun and Doctor famous for her "Little Way" of spirituality (October 1).

St. Thomas Aquinas (c. 1225-1274), Dominican philosopher, theologian, and Doctor (January 28).

St. Thomas à Becket (1118-1170), Archbishop of Canterbury and martyr (December 29).

St. Thomas More (1478-1535), Lord Chancellor of England and martyr (June 22).

St. Ulrich (890-973), Bishop of Augsburg (July 4).

St. Varus (d. 304), soldier who ministered to Christian prisoners and was martyred (October 19).

St. Veronica Guiliani (1660-1727), Poor Clare, abbess, and visionary (July 9).

St. Vincent de Paul (1580-1660), founder of the Lazarist Fathers and the Sisters of Charity (September 27).

St. Vitus (d. c. 303), convert to Christianity and martyr (June 15).

St. Zenais: perhaps St. Zenaida (first century) Jewish convert to Christianity who practiced medicine (October 11).

St. Zita (c. 1218-1278), domestic servant (April 27).

Biographical Note

~

Aloysius Roche

Aloysius Roche was born in Scotland in 1886. Ordained a Redemptorist priest, he eventually had to leave the order because of poor health, and went on to serve at Most Holy Redeemer parish in Essex, England. There he became known for his wise sermons and his simple, holy lifestyle.

Canon Roche (as he came to be called) tied current events into many of his sermons, showing how we, like the saints, can attain holiness in and through all the circumstances of our lives and our world. His writing exhibits an extensive knowledge of the lives of the saints and speaks of them with such familiarity, warmth, and charm as to bring them close to us, to teach us the simple secrets of their happiness, and to move us to become what God calls us all to be: saints in our own time.

Sophia Institute Press®

Sophia Institute® is a nonprofit institution that seeks to restore man's knowledge of eternal truth, including man's knowledge of his own nature, his relation to other persons, and his relation to God. Sophia Institute Press® serves this end in numerous ways. It publishes translations of foreign works to make them accessible to English-speaking readers, it brings back into print books that have been long out of print, and it publishes important new books that fulfill the ideals of Sophia Institute®. These books afford readers a rich source of the enduring wisdom of mankind. Sophia Institute Press® makes these high-quality books available to the public by using advanced technology and by soliciting donations to subsidize its publishing costs.

Your generosity can help provide the public with editions of works containing the enduring wisdom of the ages. Please send your tax-deductible contribution to the address below.

For your free catalog
call toll-free: **1-800-888-9344**

Sophia Institute Press®
Box 5284, Manchester, NH 03108

www.sophiainstitute.com

Sophia Institute® is a tax-exempt institution as defined by the Internal Revenue Code, Section 501(c)(3). Tax I.D. 22-2548708.